TWO-CHARACTER
PLAYS
FOR
STUDENT
ACTORS

A collection of 15
one-act plays

ROBERT MAURO

D1117116

MERIWETHER PUBLISHING LTD.
Colorado Springs, Colorado

Meriwether Publishing Ltd., Publisher
Box 7710
Colorado Springs, CO 80933

Editor: Arthur Zapel
Typesetting: Sharon Garlock
Cover design: Michelle Zapel Gallardo

© Copyright MCMLXXXVIII Meriwether Publishing Ltd.
Printed in the United States of America
First Edition

Library of Congress Cataloging-in-Publication Data

Mauro, Robert, 1946-
    Two-character plays for student actors.

    1. One-act plays.   2. Acting.   I. Title.
PN2080.M38   1988   812'.54   88-60078
ISBN 0-916260-53-4

4   5   6   7   8   99   98   97

To my teachers,
who ignited the spark.
To my parents,
who nurtured the flame.
To my friends,
who kept it burning.

INTRODUCTION

Chock full of hilarious comedies and moving dramas, *Two Character Plays for Student Actors* will tickle your funny bone and touch your heart. The sketches are rich and varied and explore the full spectrum of human emotion. In the clever dialog and creative scenes, you'll see and hear what it's like to grow old and to be young, to find love and to lose it, and to live and die for one's beliefs. The audience, whether young or old, will experience suspense, intrigue, happiness, sadness, nostalgia and, above all, hope.

The actors performing these plays will have a chance to utilize the full range of their talents, from joy to sorrow. And the many roles range from liberated women to bumbling detectives, from childhood sweethearts to senior citizens.

Therefore, whether it's comedy or tragedy, *Two Character Plays for Student Actors* is an indispensable collection of works for theatre groups and workshops, a rich source of material for auditions and readings, and a valuable training tool for acting classes everywhere. You'll find it all in *Two Character Plays for Student Actors* — mime, slapstick, modern drama, age-old tragedy, and even burlesque.

All and all, get ready to laugh and cry, sense and feel — get ready to act.

Gary Burghoff

*"Radar" on television's **M*A*S*H** series. Also starring performer of several Broadway plays and musicals including: **You're a Good Man, Charlie Brown!** and **The Nerd.***

FOREWORD

*In the following pages you will see a collection of short plays for two actors. Some of these sketches have two female characters; some have two male characters. Several plays have a male and a female in the cast. Hopefully, all of my plays have men and women in them who will make you think. That is every writer's goal: to make an audience think. Think about what is important in this short drama we are all cast into — life. The importance of understanding, love and respect for each other is what I have tried to express. And the fact that we are **all** important. For we all have one thing in common whether we're old or young, black or white, disabled or non-disabled. Humanity.*

__Two Character Plays for Student Actors__ I hope will give the men and women who act in these comedies and dramas a chance to make an audience laugh, cry and, above all, think about their lives and the lives of others. Shakespeare says in Act II, Scene VII of As You Like It, "All the world is a stage,/ And all the men and women merely players." Conversely, every stage is a small world, but a great arena for the betterment of all of us. And no actor is merely a player. He or she is a teacher. And the play is a powerful medium through which the playwright, the actors, the director and the audience all come together to learn.

Think about it . . . .

CONTENTS

PLAYS
FOR
MEN
AND
WOMEN

Uptown/Downtown

PRODUCTION NOTES

PLAYERS: 1 male; 1 female.

PLAYING TIME: About 15 minutes.

COSTUMES: Both are in jeans, but JOEY wears a black leather jacket.

PROPERTIES: Knapsack, books, two beat-up two-wheelers, red bandanna.

LIGHTING EFFECTS: None.

SOUND EFFECTS: None.

Uptown/Downtown

CHARACTERS: JOEY, a gang-leader; TAMI, a rich high-school girl.

Scene 1

TIME: Today.

SETTING: A street corner between an upper-class neighborhood and a lower-income neighborhood. A railroad track may be painted or drawn down from Backstage to Stage Front to symbolize the separation between the two cultures. On one side of the tracks is a beautiful mansion on a hill. On the other side is a rundown city housing tenement. A graffiti-covered bench is on poor side.

AT RISE: JOEY enters from the lower-class side of the tracks. He is on a beat-up old two-wheeler. He looks around.

JOEY: **Where is that girl? I knew she'd chicken out. These rich girls are all the same. They think we poor guys are all stupid.** (*He stands his bike by the bench and walks around.*) **Well, this dude is no dummy. Hey, man, I am the leader of the Young Knights. OK? And that is the coolest gang in this here town. And she's just some dumb rich kid. I knew when she promised to tutor me so I'd pass that high school exam, she was just showing off to her rich friends. They're all alike.** (*Looks at the mansion up on the hill*) **Look at that place. It must have cost some rich dude a million bucks.** (*He shakes his head.*) **They're all alike. You know. They drive around in their Mercedes and Porsches. And they think down here we're all garbage. Hey, rich girl, Joey is not garbage! You hear me? She probably drives a fifty-thousand dollar car her rich daddy bought for her sweet sixteen party. Hey, rich girl. See what I drive? I drive a beat-up old bike.** (*Points to his bike*) **See? Not even a**

– 4 –

1	ten-speed. Barely one. She needs new tires and a paint
2	job. Now where am I supposed to get the money for that?
3	Huh? Can you tell me that, rich girl? Can you? *(Pause,*
4	*then)* See! No comment. I should have quit this dumb high
5	school when I wanted to. I could have
6	been . . . been . . .something by now. But no, she says.
7	She'll help me graduate. Then I could go to college. Ha.
8	Me? Sure, sure, she says. Ha. Now why should I want to
9	go to college? Better yet, why should she want to help
10	me? They're all so rich, what do they need to help us for?
11	Beats me. I bet she pulls up in a Porsche or a Vet, if not
12	a Mercedes. *(At that moment, TAMI enters from rich-side of*
13	*town. She is on a beat-up old bike that needs a paint job.)*
14	TAMI: *(Jumping off her bike)* **Sorry I'm late, Joey.**
15	JOEY: **Hey, forget it, girl. Figured you would be.**
16	TAMI: **You did?**
17	JOEY: **Sure, girl.**
18	TAMI: **Please call me Tami.**
19	JOEY: **Right. Yeah. Sure. Tami. It's OK you're late.**
20	TAMI: **I would have been here sooner, but this dumb old**
21	**bike blew a tire. They're pretty worn, I guess. I had to**
22	**fix it.**
23	JOEY: **Oh, yeah? You fix flats?**
24	TAMI: **Sure. No sweat.**
25	JOEY: **Really?**
26	TAMI: **Really.**
27	JOEY: **All right. But, hey, you should get new ones. You could**
28	**get killed on those wheels, especially around these**
29	**railroad tracks.**
30	TAMI: **I know. But I never get a chance.**
31	JOEY: **Busy with all those proms and debutante balls up on**
32	**the hill, huh?**
33	TAMI: **No.**
34	JOEY: **No. Busy tutoring?**
35	TAMI: **Me? No. Actually I'm usually busy with my own**

1	school work. I'm not too good at school.
2	JOEY: Say what? You're not too good at school work? And
3	you're going to tutor me?
4	TAMI: Sure.
5	JOEY: Hey, I don't pay no dummy to tutor me.
6	TAMI: Pay? Who said anything about pay? This was an offer
7	you couldn't refuse. Remember? And don't call me a
8	dummy. I hate that.
9	JOEY: Oh, I suppose people do it a lot. Right?
10	TAMI: You'd be surprised.
11	JOEY: Now why would they call you a dummy?
12	TAMI: I have trouble reading.
13	JOEY: This is terrific. I have a reading tutor who can't read.
14	TAMI: Oh, I can read now.
15	JOEY: Huh?
16	TAMI: You see, I have dyslexia.
17	JOEY: What?
18	TAMI: Dyslexia.
19	JOEY: It ain't catching, is it?
20	TAMI: No.
21	JOEY: So what is this dyslexia?
22	TAMI: It's a learning disability. They call it L.D. Mainly I
23	have trouble reading and writing.
24	JOEY: Oh, yeah. Well mainly I do too. Maybe I got L.D.
25	TAMI: I don't think so.
26	JOEY: Hey, who knows, right? *(She shrugs.)* So how you going
27	to help me?
28	TAMI: Well, I learned how to read and write, so I figured if
29	I could, so could you.
30	JOEY: Is that right? You figured this out on your own?
31	TAMI: Yep. What do you think?
32	JOEY: I don't know. *(He thinks.)* So you telling me you weren't
33	kidding about doing this for nothing? You're going to do
34	this all for nothing? Is that what you're telling me?
35	TAMI: No. Not exactly.

1	**JOEY:**	**No? Here it comes.** *(Thinks)* **So . . . then what exactly?**
2		**Why exactly are you doing this?**
3	**TAMI:**	**Because I thought I could help you.**
4	**JOEY:**	**Hey, I don't need none of your charity. No way.**
5	**TAMI:**	**It's not charity. It's just that I thought I could help**
6		**you. I had a friend who helped me when most people said**
7		**I was stupid. My friend believed in me.**
8	**JOEY:**	**Look, I don't need no help from no rich girl in no old**
9		**clothes, especially one with displexia.**
10	**TAMI:**	**Dyslexia.**
11	**JOEY:**	**Yeah, that. I don't need no help. Hey, I don't even like**
12		**you.**
13	**TAMI:**	**Oh. I see.** *(She's hurt.)* **Sorry.**
14	**JOEY:**	**Oh, look. It's nothing personal, Tam, but —**
15	**TAMI:**	**No girl is going to show macho you anything.**
16	**JOEY:**	**You're mad at me. Right?**
17	**TAMI:**	**Do you need my help or not?**
18	**JOEY:**	*(Folds his arms)* **No.**
19	**TAMI:**	**You don't? But I thought you were told if you didn't**
20		**pass English, you wouldn't graduate.**
21	**JOEY:**	**So . . . it wouldn't be the first time.**
22	**TAMI:**	**You don't want me to help you — after I blew a tire**
23		**getting over here?**
24	**JOEY:**	**Who needs your charity?**
25	**TAMI:**	**Hey, buddy, I could be out with Biff and Brad —**
26	**JOEY:**	*(He laughs.)* **Biff and Brad? Who are they?**
27	**TAMI:**	**Their dad owns that mansion up there on the hill.**
28		**That Biff and Brad, they think I'm . . .** *(Thinking of*
29		*something to impress JOEY)* **. . . hot stuff.**
30	**JOEY:**	*(Laughing)* **Hot stuff, eh? Really?**
31	**TAMI:**	**Sure.**
32	**JOEY:**	**Biff and Brad, huh? With you?**
33	**TAMI:**	**Yeah. Me. Why?**
34	**JOEY:**	**You don't look like you're the Biff and Brad type.**
35	**TAMI:**	**Well . . . I am.**

1	JOEY: Oh, no. Not you, girl. You look more like the outdoor-
2	type to me. And, hey, you and I, we both know that Biff
3	and Brad are not the outdoors type.
4	TAMI: *(Thinking)* **No.**
5	JOEY: No is right. Biff and Brad like only indoor sports.
6	Right? Huh?
7	TAMI: I guess.
8	JOEY: Well, I know. Those rich guys are all alike. They like
9	fish eggs and cucumber sandwiches. And indoor sports.
10	TAMI: Oh, and you don't like . . . indoor sports?
11	JOEY: I like 'em indoors or *(Walking closer to her)* outdoors.
12	TAMI: *(Steps back shyly)* I do like camping.
13	JOEY: *(Not wanting to frighten her, backs away)* Yeah, right. And
14	I bet you like hunting and fishing.
15	TAMI: I don't like hunting.
16	JOEY: You don't?
17	TAMI: No. I really couldn't shoot anything.
18	JOEY: No?
19	TAMI: And you could?
20	JOEY: Sure. No sweat.
21	TAMI: Really?
22	JOEY: Hey, do I look like a wimp?
23	TAMI: That has nothing to do with killing a helpless animal.
24	Did you ever see "Bambi"?
25	JOEY: What's that?
26	TAMI: A movie about a little deer.
27	JOEY: Oh, you like movies, too?
28	TAMI: Yes. Do you?
29	JOEY: Sure. You ever see "Kung Fu Killers"?
30	TAMI: Not really.
31	JOEY: Figures. So you like fishing?
32	TAMI: Yes, I do. Do you?
33	JOEY: Sure. Maybe you'd like to go fishing with me
34	sometime?
35	TAMI: Well . . .

1	JOEY:	Oh, yes. I forgot. What would Biff and Brad say?
2	TAMI:	It's not that.
3	JOEY:	Then what is it?
4	TAMI:	I agreed to help you pass that English test so —
5	JOEY:	Right, business is business.
6	TAMI:	I just wanted to help.
7	JOEY:	Look, who said I needed your help? I don't need
8		anybody.
9	TAMI:	OK. But then why did you come? To make fun of my
10		clothes? To make fun of my friends?
11	JOEY:	Aha! Then you do know the popular but obnoxious
12		Biff and Brad boys?
13	TAMI:	Very funny, Joseph.
14	JOEY:	Please, call me Joey.
15	TAMI:	Joey, let's just be friends. OK?
16	JOEY:	OK. So . . . does this mean you will go to the old fishing
17		hole with me? Hmmmm? You never know what you'll
18		catch.
19	TAMI:	Joey. Be serious.
20	JOEY:	Tami. Come on. Loosen up.
21	TAMI:	Joey, we're here to learn.
22	JOEY:	I bet I could teach you a few things. *(Walks closer to*
23		*her)*
24	TAMI:	*(Backing away from him a bit)* I just wanted to tutor you.
25	JOEY:	You sure that's all? You weren't turned on by
26		my . . . old clothes?
27	TAMI:	Very cute.
28	JOEY:	That's me. At least that's what all the girls say.
29	TAMI:	I'll bet.
30	JOEY:	You mean I don't give you goose bumps?
31	TAMI:	*(She laughs.)* I'm sorry, but you're so funny.
32	JOEY:	Hey, Tam, you have a nice laugh.
33	TAMI:	That's what all the boys tell me.
34	JOEY:	I'll bet — even with those old clothes.
35	TAMI:	Hey, buddy, I like second hand clothes. OK?

1	JOEY:	They look more like third hand to me.
2	TAMI:	*(Looking at herself)* **Yeah, they do look sort of old, don't**
3		**they?**
4	JOEY:	Real old. But you look OK in them.
5	TAMI:	I do?
6	JOEY:	Sure, you do.
7	TAMI:	Thanks.
8	JOEY:	Hey, no problem. So why you want to meet me here?
9	TAMI:	Me? What do you mean me?
10	JOEY:	As in you. Like *(Spelling)* Y-O-U. You.
11	TAMI:	You can spell.
12	JOEY:	*(Spelling)* Y-E-S.
13	TAMI:	Great. How about trying antidisestablishmentarianism.
14	JOEY:	How about telling me why you wanted to meet M-E
15		here?
16	TAMI:	Joey, you wanted to meet here. I wanted to meet at
17		the library. Remember? You wanted to meet here.
18	JOEY:	Yeah, I forgot. I made a promise to my gang never to
19		be seen near a library — let alone in one. Do you know
20		what that could do to my reputation if my gang caught
21		me in a library?
22	TAMI:	Are you sure they know what a library is?
23	JOEY:	*(He laughs, then gets serious.)* Hey, of course they do.
24	TAMI:	You don't sound so sure.
25	JOEY:	I'm sure. Look, they may be stupid, but they're not
26		dumb.
27	TAMI:	So because you're afraid of what the gang would
28		think, you wanted to meet me here and not at the library?
29	JOEY:	I like it here. And I'm not afraid of no dumb gang
30		members. You got a problem with that?
31	TAMI:	Nope. It's just that if trains start passing, it's going
32		to be a little difficult to master English.
33	JOEY:	No one has to master nothing. I just have to know
34		enough to pass that crummy final exam. So when do we
35		start?

1	TAMI:	Right now if you want. I brought my books. *(She takes*
2		*them out of her knapsack.)* **See?**
3	JOEY:	**Terrific. What do we do first?**
4	TAMI:	**What are you the worst at? Reading or writing?**
5	JOEY:	**Both.**
6	TAMI:	**OK. We'll start with reading.**
7	JOEY:	**Sounds exciting.**
8	TAMI:	**To me it is.**
9	JOEY:	**To you old clothes are exciting.**
10	TAMI:	**Right. Come on, let's sit over here on the bench.**
11	JOEY:	**Sure. You want to fumigate it first?**
12	TAMI:	**It looks like it could use it.**
13	JOEY:	**You got that right.** *(He takes out a red bandanna and lays*
14		*it on the bench for her.)* **There. Sit on that.**
15	TAMI:	**Thank you.**
16	JOEY:	**No problem. It's a filthy bench. There's a lot of slobs**
17		**around here.**
18	TAMI:	**At least they like to write.**
19	JOEY:	**Yeah. All over the furniture.**
20	TAMI:	**I guess.**
21	JOEY:	**Yeah, well I know.**
22	TAMI:	**You like to write all over the furniture?**
23	JOEY:	*(Folds his arms)* **Hey, no way. No.**
24	TAMI:	**Oh. Right.** *(She opens a book.)* **We'll start with a little**
25		**poetry.**
26	JOEY:	**Poetry? Me? You've got to be kidding.**
27	TAMI:	**Nope. We'll start with Lorca.**
28	JOEY:	**Loco?**
29	TAMI:	*(Spelling)* **L-O-R-C-A — Lorca.**
30	JOEY:	**Oh. Him.**
31	TAMI:	**You know Lorca?**
32	JOEY:	**Ain't he the dude that used to have that singing group**
33		**on TV?**
34	TAMI:	**Singing group?**
35	JOEY:	**Yeah. You know. Tony O'Lorca and Dawn.** *(He laughs.)*

1	TAMI:	That was Tony Orlando and Dawn. And stop kidding
2		around. Learning is a serious business.
3	JOEY:	Oh, yeah? So what do you do for fun? Seriously.
4	TAMI:	Actually, I read. I want to get good at it. There's so
5		many beautiful things to read. And having dyslexia
6		doesn't make it easy.
7	JOEY:	Well, it isn't easy for me either. I hate it when people
8		laugh at me when I stumble over a word.
9	TAMI:	I know what you mean.
10	JOEY:	Yeah? You do?
11	TAMI:	Sure. By our age we should be reading pretty well
12		and when we can't, people laugh. It hurts. I know how
13		you feel.
14	JOEY:	Yeah. You know, Tam, I think you do.
15	TAMI:	I do.
16	JOEY:	Yeah.
17	TAMI:	Yes.
18	JOEY:	You sure?
19	TAMI:	Yes. Joey, come on. Let's start. And I promise no
20		matter how much you stumble, I won't laugh. I promise.
21		So let's read.
22	JOEY:	Do we have to?
23	TAMI:	Look, do you want me to tutor you or not?
24	JOEY:	I'd rather take you fishing.
25	TAMI:	No way.
26	JOEY:	So back to business, right?
27	TAMI:	Right.
28	JOEY:	You like digging for worms?
29	TAMI:	Are you kidding?
30	JOEY:	No. Why would I kid you? I just get the feeling Biff
31		and Brad would hate digging for worms. They'd probably
32		buy 'em by the dozen in some gourmet fishing store, but
33		not you.
34	TAMI:	Why not me?
35	JOEY:	I just have this feeling you love digging for worms.

1	TAMI:	Well . . .
2	JOEY:	*(Pointing at her)* **See! I knew it. You love it!**
3	TAMI:	**You're wrong. I don't exactly love it.**
4	JOEY:	**But you don't exactly hate it.**
5	TAMI:	**No . . . I don't.**
6	JOEY:	**Hey, terrific. Let's chuck your books and go dig for**
7		**worms.**
8	TAMI:	**I don't believe this. I came here to tutor you.**
9	JOEY:	**I got it. I'll dig for worms, while you read me poetry.**
10	TAMI:	**You won't laugh at me if I stumble over a word?**
11	JOEY:	**Tami, hey, this is Joey. I would never do that to my**
12		**friend.**
13	TAMI:	**Great. But first I dig for worms while *you* read for me.**
14	JOEY:	**You'll laugh.**
15	TAMI:	**Joey, I'd never laugh at a friend.**
16	JOEY:	**No? You promise?**
17	TAMI:	**It depends.**
18	JOEY:	**Oh, yeah? On what?**
19	TAMI:	**On how big your worms are. I'll race you to the lake.**
20		*(They get up, and race off laughing as the curtain falls.)*
21		
22		
23		
24		
25		
26		
27		
28		
29		
30		
31		
32		
33		
34		
35		

Joan

PRODUCTION NOTES

PLAYERS: 1 male; 1 female.

PLAYING TIME: About 12 minutes.

COSTUMES: JOAN is in man's white shirt and mail pants of the period. The PRIEST is in black with black cloak.

PROPERTIES: A candle.

LIGHTING EFFECTS: Lights can dim out and a spotlight comes up on PRIEST.

SOUND EFFECTS: None.

Joan

CHARACTERS: JOAN D'ARC, the maid of Orleans; A PRIEST.

Scene 1

TIME: May 29, 1431, the day before her execution.

SETTING: A prison cell. Shadow of bars from a small window are silhouetted on the rear wall. There is a small crude table and two crude chairs. A lighted candle sits on the table.

AT RISE: JOAN is sitting in one chair. A long chain runs from the wall to her leg. The PRIEST stands with his back to JOAN. His hands are folded in prayer.

JOAN: So I am to die tomorrow?

PRIEST: Yes. I fear it has been decided.

JOAN: I should have guessed it would be.

PRIEST: It is God's will.

JOAN: Don't blame it on God. Everybody blames everything on him.

PRIEST: *(Turning to face her)* Are you saying then it is not God's will?

JOAN: It is more likely the wishes of men.

PRIEST: Who speak for God.

JOAN: Who at least presume to.

PRIEST: *(At a loss for words)* As you say.

JOAN: *(After a pause)* Father?

PRIEST: Yes, Joan?

JOAN: Does it hurt to be burned at the stake?

PRIEST: *(Turning away from her)* Joan, must we talk of that?

JOAN: *(She shrugs.)* I was just curious. Will I suffer much? Or will I just —

PRIEST: *(Turning towards her)* Must we talk of this?

JOAN: I was just curious. OK? I've never been burned at the

1 **stake before.** *(She puts her hand over the candle flame.)*

2 **PRIEST:** *(Pulling her hand away)* **What are you doing?**

3 **JOAN:** **Just testing. As I told you, I am curious.**

4 **PRIEST:** **Too curious, I suspect. Did you burn yourself?**

5 **JOAN:** *(Rubbing her hand)* **No. It was hot though. But you**
6 **pulled my hand away before I was burned. Will you do**
7 **that tomorrow, Father?**

8 **PRIEST:** *(Not wanting to answer)* **Can we speak of more**
9 **pleasant things?**

10 **JOAN:** **Such as?**

11 **PRIEST:** **The weather.**

12 **JOAN:** *(Laughing)* **The ... weather?**

13 **PRIEST:** **It is a lovely day.**

14 **JOAN:** **Yes? Really?** *(She goes to Stage Left and stands on her*
15 *tiptoes.)* **I cannot see out my only window. What month is**
16 **it?**

17 **PRIEST:** **It is May.**

18 **JOAN:** *(Still stretching, trying to look out the high window)* **Oh,**
19 **wait. I can see the sky. It does look quite blue.**

20 **PRIEST:** **A glorious day. You should hear the birds singing.**

21 **JOAN:** *(She stands with her arms folded.)* **I fear I'll be hearing**
22 **plenty of doves quite soon.** *(She shivers.)*

23 **PRIEST:** **Are you cold, Joan?** *(He goes to give her his cloak.)*

24 **JOAN:** **As death.** *(He stops and she goes to sit down.)* **It is damp**
25 **and cold in here. And there are no birds singing.**

26 **PRIEST:** **I fear not.** *(He sits on a chair on the other side of the*
27 *table.)* **Do you wish to confess your sins?**

28 **JOAN:** **I'd rather talk about the weather.**

29 **PRIEST:** **Ah, yes. Well, it is —**

30 **JOAN:** *(Finishing for him)* **A glorious day.**

31 **PRIEST:** **Truly.**

32 **JOAN:** **I used to love playing in the leaves when I was a little**
33 **girl. Every autumn we'd rake them into great piles. Then**
34 **run across the meadow and jump into them. It**
35 **was ... glorious.**

1 PRIEST: Yes.

2 JOAN: Did you play in the leaves when you were a little

3 child, Father?

4 PRIEST: *(He thinks.)* I imagine so. But it was so long ago.

5 Still ... I imagine I did. I and my brothers and sisters.

6 JOAN: Were there many?

7 PRIEST: Leaves?

8 JOAN: No. Brothers and sisters.

9 PRIEST: Ah, indeed. Eight.

10 JOAN: Eight. Really? I have three brothers and one sister.

11 PRIEST: All soldiers?

12 JOAN: No.

13 PRIEST: What are their names?

14 JOAN: There is Jacquemin, Pierre, Jean and my sister

15 Catherine. Catherine died as a child. What are the names

16 of your brothers and sisters?

17 PRIEST: There is Jacque, Peter, Christopher, Marie,

18 Jacqueline, Noel, Daniel and myself.

19 JOAN: A large family is so nice.

20 PRIEST: Except when we fought over the milk and the

21 bread, as children will.

22 JOAN: Yes. So where are they now? Are there any more

23 priests in the family?

24 PRIEST: No. Just me. But my sister Jacqueline is a nun.

25 JOAN: Ah. Your mother and father must be proud.

26 PRIEST: I guess.

27 JOAN: What? They are not?

28 PRIEST: They seem happier with my brothers who are

29 soldiers.

30 JOAN: Soldiers? You mean like me? *(He nods.)* **Really?**

31 PRIEST: *(He nods.)* **Yes.** *(Whispering to her)* **My mother thinks**

32 **you are wonderful.**

33 JOAN: God bless all our mothers.

34 PRIEST: *(Blessing himself)* **Truly.**

35 JOAN: And your father, Father? What does he think?

1   **PRIEST:** *(He stands and walks to Stage Front and faces audience.)*
2   **Not so wonderful.**
3   **JOAN:**   I see. Well, I am young. I admit to being unliked.
4   **PRIEST:**   He says all women should —
5   **JOAN:**   *(Finishing for him)* **Have eight children, preferably all**
6   **soldiers?**
7   **PRIEST:**   *(Pointing at her)* **Amazing! How did you guess?**
8   **JOAN:**   When you're nineteen years old and about to be
9   burned at the stake for wearing men's clothes, it isn't
10   difficult.
11   **PRIEST:**   Yes. Well, I fear you will not go to your final reward
12   unless you confess. And dress as a woman.
13   **JOAN:**   I dress as the soldier I am.
14   **PRIEST:**   Then you will not confess?
15   **JOAN:**   Confess what? That I fought for what I thought was
16   best for my country? That I led my men as best I could
17   for the glory of France and God? I will confess that. But
18   I fear that is not the confession you are looking for.
19   **PRIEST:**   No.
20   **JOAN:**   As a result, I fear I will still be burned. *(She puts her*
21   *hand over the flame and the PRIEST takes the candle away.)*
22   **PRIEST:**   Stop that! It is a sin to abuse yourself in such a
23   manner.
24   **JOAN:**   Sorry. I just don't like surprises. I wanted a taste of
25   what's in store for me tomorrow. Have they decided on
26   a time yet?
27   **PRIEST:**   *(Shrugs)* They don't tell me those things. It's just,
28   "Father, go hear the prisoner's confession." Or, "Father,
29   do this." Or, "Father, do that." I'm never told anything
30   about the executions.
31   **JOAN:**   Have there been many.
32   **PRIEST:**   You'd be surprised.
33   **JOAN:**   I sort of doubt that. So they don't tell you much
34   either?
35   **PRIEST:**   No. All they tell me is to pray. It's not a very

1   demanding career.

2 JOAN: Well, Father ... *(Walks over to him, patting him on the*
3 *back)* I'm sure it's not easy listening to the confessions of
4 those who are about to be barbequed. I guess most are
5 pretty upset about the whole thing.

6 PRIEST: To say the least. It seems these days no one is in a
7 hurry to go to their final reward.

8 JOAN: Why would they be with such glorious weather?

9 PRIEST: This is true. Perhaps if it rained a bit more often.

10 JOAN: Yes, perhaps. But then God does move in mysterious
11 ways.

12 PRIEST: This is true.

13 JOAN: Still, rain would at least make it seem all the more
14 apropos.

15 PRIEST: Perhaps.

16 JOAN: Nevertheless, I sort of doubt that, too. One is never
17 in a rush for the ax or the stake — rain or shine.

18 PRIEST: I would imagine so.

19 JOAN: *(She sits.)* Take it from one who knows first hand. They
20 are not.

21 PRIEST: As you say. *(Putting the candle on the table)* Now no
22 more playing with fire.

23 JOAN: I fear I've done too much of that already.

24 PRIEST: Will you confess then and cleanse your soul of this
25 sin?

26 JOAN: Can I be honest with you, Father?

27 PRIEST: Then you will confess?

28 JOAN: I wasn't talking about confessing. What I meant was
29 I'd like to talk about my feelings about all this.

30 PRIEST: All what?

31 JOAN: This. My trial. My sentence. My execution.

32 PRIEST: Must we be morbid?

33 JOAN: It's certainly not my choice. *(She stands and paces.)* But
34 since it has been as they say, thrust upon me, *(To his face)*
35 I'll be as morbid as I have to be to make my point. OK?

1 PRIEST: *(Backing away a bit)* **As you wish.**
2 JOAN: *(Pacing)* **As I wish? I wish I were back in that lovely**
3   **autumn meadow of my childhood jumping into those big**
4   **piles of leaves. But since that was then and this is now . . .**
5   *(To his face again)* **and since I'm about to be barbequed,**
6   **I'd like to set the record straight. OK?**
7 PRIEST: **In the form of a confession?**
8 JOAN: **NO! In the form of a protest! A diatribe! A chewing**
9   **out! A criticism, if you will.**
10 PRIEST: **If you will it.**
11 JOAN: **I sure do will it.** *(Paces as she talks)* **First off, they are**
12   **not burning me out of any little problem with me dressing**
13   **up in men's clothes. What a laugh.**
14 PRIEST: **This is no laughing matter.**
15 JOAN: **No? Watch me.** *(She laughs, then seriously)* **To continue.**
16 PRIEST: **Please do.**
17 JOAN: **I do please. I am being burned not for being dressed**
18   **as a man, but for having the courage to *act* as one. To**
19   **stand up and fight for what I felt was right, for what was**
20   **my duty, for what my God would have me do.**
21 PRIEST: **You dare assume to know what God thinks?**
22 JOAN: **I know a lot of you men who do that and I don't see**
23   **any of you being barbequed for it. Most of you become**
24   **saints, if you know what I mean.**
25 PRIEST: **I think you assume too much.**
26 JOAN: **You might be right. But I know what my heart tells**
27   **me and is it not through our hearts that God speaks to**
28   **us? Isn't that what you all say?**
29 PRIEST: **Well — you also say God spoke to you in French**
30   **and not in English.**
31 JOAN: *(She laughs ironically)* **I am French.** *(She shrugs.)* **I guess**
32   **he figured I'd catch on faster if he spoke my language. Is**
33   **that a sin?**
34 PRIEST: **Well —**
35 JOAN: **Well, well, well. Confess it. It is a sin to you English**

1   who have captured me.

2 PRIEST: *(Whispering)* Not to me. I think —

3 JOAN: Unfortunately, it's not important what we little

4   people think, Father.

5 PRIEST: I have often heard that.

6 JOAN: So if you ask me why I am being burned tomorrow,

7   I will tell you. Do you ask?

8 PRIEST: What?

9 JOAN: Do you want to know the real reason I am going to

10   be barbequed tomorrow?

11 PRIEST: I have this strange feeling you will tell me whether

12   or not I wish to hear it.

13 JOAN: Yes. You are right, Father. You know me well.

14 PRIEST: *(Whispering to her)* It is an honor. *(Louder)* Then you

15   will confess?

16 JOAN: *(Whispering)* To God I will. *(Louder)* Is it not your lot

17   in life to hear the final ravings of those of us who are

18   about to be *(Still louder)* barbequed for reasons of state?

19 PRIEST: *(In a near whisper)* We all have our crosses to bear.

20 JOAN: We do indeed. *(Puts her hand over flame again)* Or our

21   flames.

22 PRIEST: *(Pulling candle away from her)* And still you won't

23   confess?

24 JOAN: You want my confession?

25 PRIEST: It would lighten both our hearts.

26 JOAN: *(She sits in chair.)* OK, OK. Here it is. You want to take

27   notes?

28 PRIEST: That is not necessary. It will be between you, me

29   and God.

30 JOAN: Yes. And the five guards your king has placed outside

31   my door. I guess they fear the little maid of Orleans more

32   than I thought.

33 PRIEST: *(Whispering to her)* They do.

34 JOAN: I guessed as much.

35 PRIEST: So . . .

1	JOAN:	So I confess I did dress up as a man. But only because
2		they aren't in the habit of making armor for women these
3		days. Maybe some day, but not in the fifteenth century.
4		Also, I confess I did take up arms. I did slay many in
5		battle. I did wage war. I did all these things. Although
6		we never fought on Sundays.
7	PRIEST:	I have heard.
8	JOAN:	Sunday is God's day and I did all these things for . . .
9		*(She stops and thinks.)*
10	PRIEST:	Yes . . . For whom did you do all these things, Joan?
11	JOAN:	You see. That's the funny thing, Father. I did them
12		for my king, my country and my God. You think I made
13		the right choice?
14	PRIEST:	It is not for me to say.
15	JOAN:	Right. Now everyone is mum. Mum's the word. Let
16		the girl burn. Do not stand up and defend her. Do not be
17		a man. Do not protest too loudly . . . *(In his face)* Or at all.
18	PRIEST:	I am just a priest.
19	JOAN:	I am just a girl.
20	PRIEST:	As you say.
21	JOAN:	What does it matter what I say? Tomorrow I will be
22		barbequed and my ashes will be scattered to the four
23		winds. And that will be that for little Joan of Domremy,
24		France. Right. Father?
25	PRIEST:	One can never tell. God moves in mysterious ways.
26	JOAN:	As you say.
27	PRIEST:	So is that it?
28	JOAN:	Is that what?
29	PRIEST:	Your confession?
30	JOAN:	If you like.
31	PRIEST:	Joan, it's not for me to decide. It's for you to decide.
32	JOAN:	I prefer to sit and wait. I am cold and tired. I just
33		want to get it over with. I just hope everyone has a good
34		time at the barbeque tomorrow. I know I used to love
35		them. Of course, at those we were usually cooking a pig

1   and not a person, but then I suppose if you were a pig
2   you were not amused.
3 PRIEST: I would think not.
4 JOAN: Me, too. They sure squealed a lot. Guess I will too.
5 PRIEST: Joan!
6 JOAN: Sorry, sorry. I just keep thinking about those flames.
7   I'll try to think of those great piles of leaves back home
8   in Domremy, or maybe I'll think of the sunshine
9   tomorrow. I have this feeling it's going to be a glorious
10   day.
11 PRIEST: As you say.
12 JOAN: Yes. My heart tells me it will be.
13 PRIEST: *(The lights dim out and a spotlight comes up on the*
14   *PRIEST, who walks up front to stand before the audience.)* **After**
15   **it was all over, the executioner claimed there was nothing**
16   **left of Joan — nothing at all, except her heart. That, said**
17   **the executioner, would not burn.** *(He shrugs.)* **Who's to**
18   **believe a demented, probably drunken, executioner?** *(He*
19   *smiles, points to himself and whispers to audience.)* **Me.** *(Lights*
20   *dim out as the curtain falls.)*
21
22
23
24
25
26
27
28
29
30
31
32
33
34
35

Going Down!

PRODUCTION NOTES

PLAYERS: 1 male; 1 female.

PLAYING TIME: About 15 minutes.

COSTUMES: SUZIE wears a business suit with skirt, high heels and glasses. CLARK wears a business suit, no glasses.

PROPERTIES: Man's attaché case, woman's attaché case, note pad.

LIGHTING EFFECTS: Lights blink out for a few seconds so sign reading *13th Floor* can be replaced with sign reading *1st Floor.*

SOUND EFFECTS: Sound of elevator bell to indicate elevator has reached floor.

Going Down!

CHARACTERS: SUZIE WINNER, the new boss; CLARK SAUNDERS, a male-chauvinist pig

Scene 1

TIME: Nearly Midnight.

SETTING: The setting suggests a floor in a large Manhattan corporate office building. A sign hanging above the elevator says DATA SYSTEMS UNLIMITED. There is the button of an elevator and a sign on the wall next to the elevator. The sign says 13th FLOOR.

AT RISE: SUZIE WINNER walks up to the elevator from Stage Left. She carries an attaché case.

SUZIE: *(Looking at her watch)* **Eleven-forty-five.** *(She shakes her head.)* **I should be home in bed. I have so many people to meet tomorrow.** *(She smiles.)* **But, hey, that's what being a new corporate executive is all about. Imagine. Me. The new boss of Data Systems Unlimited. And I'm glad that so far not one of those male execs has called me babe. I absolutely detest being called that. It's so condescending. All I can say is the first guy who dares to address me as "babe" is a dead duck.** *(CLARK enters Stage Right.)*

CLARK: **Hi, babe. Work late, too, eh?**

SUZIE: *(Ready to explode)* **WHY —**

CLARK: **Whoa! Easy. Relax. So you worked late and you're beat. Don't get mad at me. Get mad at those corporate slave drivers downstairs.**

SUZIE: **Who?**

CLARK: **The bosses. So relax. You're just a little tired, babe.**

SUZIE: *(Trying desperately to control herself)* **Yes. Yes. I guess I'm just a little . . . t-tired.**

CLARK: **Get used to it. You work late often?**

1   SUZIE: Yes. You?

2   CLARK: You kidding? Me? I work late as little as possible. I

3   have managed to use every excuse in the book to get out

4   of working late. Sick wife. Sick kid.

5   SUZIE: So you're married?

6   CLARK: *(Cornering her)* Now what gave you that idea?

7   SUZIE: You just mentioned your wife and child.

8   CLARK: Oh, babe, that's just an excuse I use to get out of

9   staying here late. *(Paces around)* What a company. I've

10   been here three months and since seven this morning.

11   That's nearly sixteen hours and still no raise. What do

12   they want from me? Blood?

13   SUZIE: I don't think they want that. Do you?

14   CLARK: You bet I do! I was supposed to get a raise when

15   the new boss was hired. But did I?

16   SUZIE: Did you?

17   CLARK: Again you're kidding. Again she's kidding. Right? I

18   haven't even met the bimbo yet — no offense.

19   SUZIE: Well . . .

20   CLARK: *(Pushing the elevator button impatiently)* Where is that

21   darn elevator?

22   SUZIE: That's what I'd like to know. *(Checks her watch)* It's

23   getting late, and I have to get home.

24   CLARK: You? Me! I'm bushed. All I know is that I work my

25   brains out for this company — at least that's what I make

26   them think — and do I get any thanks — like a raise?

27   SUZIE: Do you?

28   CLARK: N-O. This has got to be the cheapest multi-billion

29   dollar corporation in the history of the world. No. The

30   history of the universe. Where is that elevator? I'd take

31   the stairs if we weren't on the — what floor is this?

32   SUZIE: Thirteenth.

33   CLARK: Yeah, right. Thirteenth. My lucky number. *(Checks*

34   *his watch)* Come on elevator. Come on.

35   SUZIE: Sounds like you're in a big hurry.

1	CLARK: Right. I have to meet the new boss tomorrow
2	morning. Another real jerk, I'll bet. A woman, I hear — oh,
3	no offense!
4	SUZIE: *(Looking him in the eye, then ironically)* **None taken.**
5	CLARK: *(Not so sure no offense was taken, then)* **All I mean is**
6	**that all of these new women execs are really the pits.**
7	**Right?**
8	SUZIE: **You think so?**
9	CLARK: **Aren't they? Each and every one?**
10	SUZIE: **Well —**
11	CLARK: **Look, all I know, babe, is this so-called woman**
12	**named Weiner — a real weiner, I'll bet — must be a real**
13	**dog. They usually are.**
14	SUZIE: **I thought her name was Winner.**
15	CLARK: **It is, but I call her weiner. Funny, eh?**
16	SUZIE: **Hilarious. But how can you be so sure she's a weiner,**
17	**as you say?**
18	CLARK: **I mean, aren't they all?**
19	SUZIE: **I —**
20	CLARK: **Look. They are. Take my word for it, babe. These**
21	**new yuppie bimbos all think they're so cool.**
22	SUZIE: **I really think —**
23	CLARK: *(Looking at her)* **Hey, you're new around here?**
24	SUZIE: **Yes, I am the —**
25	CLARK: *(Cutting her off)* **I knew it.** *(Cornering her)* **I know all**
26	**the gals around here, except you. What's your name, babe?**
27	SUZIE: *(Slipping out of the corner, then about to say SUZIE)* **Su-**
28	**Sal-Sally . . .**
29	CLARK: *(Checking his watch)* **You don't sound so sure.**
30	SUZIE: **I am positive about one thing.**
31	CLARK: **Good for you. Most women can't make up their**
32	**minds about their lipstick, let alone their name. Where**
33	**is that elevator?! So . . . What did you say your name was?**
34	SUZIE: **Su . . . er . . . Sally.**
35	CLARK: **Hi, Sal.** *(Puts his hand on her shoulder)* **Clark Saunders.**

1   *(He looks her over.)*

2   **SUZIE:** *(Pulls away, then ironically)* **Nice to meet you, Mr.**
3   **Saunders.**

4   **CLARK:** *(Moving in on her again)* **Hey, you don't sound so sure,**
5   **babe. And it's Clarkie to you. So are you or aren't you**
6   **sure about meeting me?**

7   **SUZIE:** *(Slipping away)* **You'd be surprised.**

8   **CLARK: Not really. I know women like a book. You're all the**
9   **same.**

10   **SUZIE: We are, are we?**

11   **CLARK: Every one of you. Sure, you're pretty good at taking**
12   **orders, but no good at all at giving them.**

13   **SUZIE: We're not?**

14   **CLARK: No, way. That's why you make such good**
15   **secretaries, but such terrible bosses. You can usually take**
16   **dictation, but you can't give it.**

17   **SUZIE: I see.**

18   **CLARK: So,** *(Trying to corner her)* **Sal, plan on working here**
19   **long?**

20   **SUZIE: Yes.** *(Smiling)* **You?**

21   **CLARK: I guess. I've been here since I got out of college. It's**
22   **been about three months, but seems a lot longer.**

23   **SUZIE: So you went to college.**

24   **CLARK: Yep. Graduated** *summer cum lauder.* **That's Greek**
25   **for I had a lot of women . . . friends, if you catch my drift.**

26   **SUZIE: I think I do.** *(Backing away)*

27   **CLARK:** *(Moving closer)* **Good. Maybe we can get together real**
28   **soon.**

29   **SUZIE: Oh, sooner than you think.**

30   **CLARK: Really?**

31   **SUZIE: Really.**

32   **CLARK: All right. You're all right, babe.**

33   **SUZIE: I hope you feel that way tomorrow.**

34   **CLARK: Tomorrow? So soon? Dinner and you-know-what?**

35   **SUZIE: Oh, we'll be together long before dinner.**

1	CLARK:	I can't wait babe.
2	SUZIE:	You were saying something about a raise?
3	CLARK:	Yeah. You'd think it's about time for a raise, but
4		noooooo. Not this company. Take my word for it, babe,
5		the bosses around here are the pits. Don't ever forget
6		that, Sally baby. And the women execs are the worst!
7		Never ever forget that.
8	SUZIE:	Oh, don't you worry, Clarkie. I'll remember not to.
9	CLARK:	You do that.
10	SUZIE:	*(Takes out a note pad and writes it down)* **Oh, I will. I'll**
11		**even make a note that Mr. Clark Saunders said it —**
12	CLARK:	Hey, don't let that get around!
13	SUZIE:	No. It'll be between just you and me.
14	CLARK:	Good.
15	SUZIE:	*(Writing as she talks)* "The bosses around here are the
16		pits — especially the women —"
17	CLARK:	Bimbos.
18	SUZIE:	*(Writing)* "Bimbos."
19	CLARK:	According to Clark Saunders, they're the pits.
20	SUZIE:	"According to Clark Saunders, they are the pits." I'll
21		underline that. *(She does, then puts the pad away.)*
22	CLARK:	As in armpits — with a capital "A". So we're going
23		to see each other tomorrow?
24	SUZIE:	For sure.
25	CLARK:	Terrific. You work on the thirteenth floor?
26	SUZIE:	No. The first.
27	CLARK:	*(Backing away a bit)* The first? That's where all the
28		executive offices are.
29	SUZIE:	Yes. As a matter of fact, you're right.
30	CLARK:	Oh, poor baby. You must be one of the executive
31		secretaries.
32	SUZIE:	And what do you do, Clark?
33	CLARK:	I'm a programmer. Hate it, but the money is great.
34		Hey, don't let the boss hear that.
35	SUZIE:	You must work real hard. You're here so late.

1	CLARK: Not really. I was working on this dating program I
2	wrote.
3	SUZIE: Dating program?
4	CLARK: Shush! Not so loud. We're not supposed to be using
5	the company's computer for our own use.
6	SUZIE: You could get fired for that.
7	CLARK: Right. But no one will know but us. You see, I've
8	been working on a program that feeds the records of all
9	the single gals in this company through a selection
10	matrix.
11	SUZIE: To do what?
12	CLARK: To see who is the richest, youngest, and where they
13	live.
14	SUZIE: I thought all that data was confidential.
15	CLARK: It is. I'm surprised I didn't find you in there, Sal,
16	but I did find that new bimbo.
17	SUZIE: You mean ...
18	CLARK: *(Trying to corner her)* Yep ... Ms. Suzie Winner. Hey,
19	not bad.
20	SUZIE: Really?
21	CLARK: Really. Surprising. She's pretty smart — for a
22	woman, single, but, with my luck, she probably looks like
23	a blimp. *(Puffs out his cheeks)*
24	SUZIE: You think so?
25	CLARK: They always do. Some even have mustaches. Like
26	her, I'll bet. But who needs her *(Trying to corner her)* when
27	I have you. Right?
28	SUZIE: *(Pulling away as elevator bell sounds)* **Ah, here's the**
29	**elevator.**
30	CLARK: Finally. *(They get on it.)*
31	SUZIE: Going down, Clark?
32	CLARK: If you are, babe.
33	SUZIE: Yes. I have to schedule an early appointment for
34	tomorrow.
35	CLARK: How early, babe, eh?

1	SUZIE:	How early do you get here, Clark?
2	CLARK:	Tomorrow? I'm coming in late tomorrow. I'm calling
3		in that my car broke down. I want to sleep late. So I'll
4		wander in ... say ... around twelve — in time for lunch.
5	SUZIE:	Good. I'll schedule that appointment for twelve-o-
6		one.
7	CLARK:	Twelve-o-one? *(Lights go out.)* What was that?
8	SUZIE:	Relax. Just a power failure. The emergency power
9		generator will kick in in a second. *(The sign saying*
10		*THIRTEENTH FLOOR is changed to FIRST FLOOR, then*
11		*lights come on and the elevator bell sounds.)* **Ah, there we are.**
12		And here we are on the first floor.
13	CLARK:	*(They get off elevator.)* What office you in, babe?
14	SUZIE:	The bimbo's.
15	CLARK:	The bimbo's?
16	SUZIE:	You know, the new boss.
17	CLARK:	Oh, *that* bimbo?
18	SUZIE:	Yep. That bimbo.
19	CLARK:	Geez, you work for her?
20	SUZIE:	Not exactly.
21	CLARK:	Not exactly? Then *what* exactly, *(Trying to corner her)*
22		babe? And what appointment do you have to schedule at
23		twelve-o-one tomorrow? Hummmm? You can tell Clarkie.
24	SUZIE:	Well, Clarkie, you see, I have to schedule an
25		appointment that I wouldn't miss for the whole world.
26		The whole universe.
27	CLARK:	Wow. Sounds important.
28	SUZIE:	Well, it's not really, as you say, important — but it's
29		going to be a heck of a lot of fun. Fact is, it's going to
30		make my day.
31	CLARK:	And does that have something to do with us, babe?
32		Hummm?
33	SUZIE:	*(Pulling away)* You got that right, babe.
34	CLARK:	Lunch, and ... er ... then ...
35	SUZIE:	Not exactly.

1	**CLARK:** Then what exactly? Tell me? The suspense is killing
2	me!
3	**SUZIE:** Well, Clark, I'm the bimbo?
4	**CLARK:** *(Backing away, scared)* **The ... bimbo?**
5	**SUZIE:** *The* **bimbo.**
6	**CLARK:** You mean *(Pointing at her)* you're *the* bimbo! Er, the
7	new boss?
8	**SUZIE:** That's me.
9	**CLARK:** And the appointment you want to schedule for
10	twelve-o-one tomorrow is ...
11	**SUZIE:** The one at which I AM GOING TO FIRE YOU, YOU
12	**JERK!** *(Curtain falls as SUZIE folds her arms and CLARK*
13	*slumps to the ground.)*
14	
15	
16	
17	
18	
19	
20	
21	
22	
23	
24	
25	
26	
27	
28	
29	
30	
31	
32	
33	
34	
35	

The Park Bench

PRODUCTION NOTES

CHARACTERS: 1 male; 1 female.

PLAYING TIME: About 25 minutes.

COSTUMES: The OLD MAN wears a T-shirt with the words *Sexy Senior Citizen* on it. The OLD WOMAN has on a summer dress.

PROPERTIES: Saxophone with carrying case, bag with partially knitted sweater in it, wallet, photo, umbrella, glasses, handkerchief.

SOUND EFFECTS: The OLD WOMAN's romantic saxophone solo, a siren, a pigeon cooing.

LIGHTING EFFECTS: Gray day to bright sunshine.

The Park Bench

CHARACTERS: Old man; Old woman.

Scene 1

TIME: Afternoon on a summer's day.

SETTING: Central Park. Center stage there is a park bench. City skyline backstage above and behind the trees.

AT RISE: OLD WOMAN enters from Stage Right. She carries a saxophone case in one hand and a bag containing her knitting in the other hand. She puts the saxophone case under the bench. She then dusts the bench off with a handkerchief and finally sits on the bench. She puts on her glasses, takes out her knitting, smiles contentedly and begins to knit. OLD MAN enters from Stage Right. He carries an umbrella. He looks up and holds his hand out to see if it's raining. He goes over and sits on park bench. The OLD WOMAN moves away from him, putting a safe distance between them.

OLD MAN: *(Checks again to see if it's raining, then to OLD WOMAN)* **Funny weather we're having these days. One minute it's sunshine and the next minute it's pouring cats and dogs.** *(She continues to knit.)* **But then it is that time of the year. You can never really tell what's going to happen next. The city is a very strange place with strange weather and strange . . .** *(He sees her giving him a suspicious look)* **people in it. Fortunately, or unfortunately, I am not strange. I'm sure you're not either. No. Not us.** *(She goes back to her knitting.)* **Yes sir. We're just two old folks spending a summer afternoon in the park. You're just you and I'm just me. Two ordinary old geezers. That's us.** *(She nods her head as if to say, "Sure, sure.")* **But the weather . . . now that is another story. It is strange. When I was a boy, if there was one thing you could count on, it was**

1   the weather. Yep. You could always count on the weather.
2   I mean, you knew what is was going to do. There were
3   no surprises. If it was summer, it was hot. If it was winter,
4   it was cold. If it was spring, there were buds on the trees.
5   If it was fall, there were leaves on the ground. Not
6   anymore. The whole world has been turned topsy turvy,
7   or at least tipped. I can't figure any of this world we live
8   in out. Can you? *(She ignores him.)* Well, I sure can't. Even
9   the weather reports are different. You used to get: *(He
10   imitates weather man.)* "There'll be rain today with
11   temperatures in the 80's." But not these days. Now you
12   get wind-chills, frost warnings, satellite pictures, and
13   temperatures in celsius. Summer isn't summer when they
14   tell you it's going to be thirty-eight degrees celsius. What
15   the dickens does that mean? Don't ask me. You know?
16   *(She is silent.)* Well, just give me good old fahrenheit any
17   day and I'll be as happy as a bug in a rug. By the
18   way . . . did I tell you they are saying we're heading for
19   another ice age? What do you think? *(She doesn't even look
20   at him.)* No comment, huh? Well, it's true. They all say it.
21   Even National Geographic or was it Jacque Cousteau?
22   All I know is someone said it. They sure as shootin' did.
23   So break out the mink coat, old girl. Another ice age is
24   on the way. That's what I hear. *(He twiddles his thumbs,
25   then)* So . . . what are you doing out in the park? *(She knits.)*
26   Besides knitting, I mean. I do see you like to knit. *(She
27   says nothing.)* Waiting for the rain? I have an umbrella in
28   case we need it. Be prepared. That's my motto. Or is it
29   the boy scout's? Well, it's someone's. Might as well be
30   mine. *(She still says nothing, but knits faster. He waves a hand
31   in front of her face.)* Hello. Can you hear me? Testing, one,
32   two, three. I know. Your hearing aid batteries are dead
33   and the grandkids were too busy watching MTV to run
34   down to the local five-and-ten store and buy you a new set.
35 **OLD WOMAN:**   *(Looking at him)* No. That is not it. I do not

1   wear a hearing aid. And I do not have grandchildren who
2   watch MTV. In fact, I have no grandchildren.
3   OLD MAN: Aha! You can talk.
4   OLD WOMAN: Yes. When I have something intelligent to say.
5   OLD MAN: Neither do I.
6   OLD WOMAN: Neither do you what?
7   OLD MAN: I mean, I don't have grandchildren either. I never
8   married. How about you? Ever get hitched?
9   OLD WOMAN: Really. I don't see where that's any of your
10   business.
11   OLD MAN: Actually, it isn't any of my business at all, but I
12   was curious and asking questions helps get the
13   conversation going. And this one doesn't seem to be going
14   anywhere. But for the record, I never married. Neither
15   did you. Right? I can tell.
16   OLD WOMAN: You can? Now how can you do that?
17   OLD MAN: It's all in the eyes. Your's have that look.
18   OLD WOMAN: What look?
19   OLD MAN: *(Looking into her eyes)* The look of someone who
20   almost got married, but didn't.
21   OLD WOMAN: *(Realizing he is right, then ironically)* You're so
22   smart.
23   OLD MAN: So I was right, huh?
24   OLD WOMAN: I never said that.
25   OLD MAN: Well, whatever. *(He looks around.)* I do like coming
26   to the park. There's so much you can do. Jog around the
27   lake, go for a rowboat ride, walk your dog. Do you have
28   a dog?
29   OLD WOMAN: No. I'm allergic to animal hair.
30   OLD MAN: I had a girlfriend like that once. She'd sneeze at
31   the mere mention of a dog or cat.
32   OLD WOMAN: I know the feeling. *(She sneezes.)*
33   OLD MAN: I see. Gesundheit.
34   OLD WOMAN: *(Not taking her eyes off her knitting)* Thank you.
35   OLD MAN: You're welcome. Anyway, I do like coming to the

1   park. There's so much to do. Know what I like to do most?

2   OLD WOMAN: I'm afraid to ask.

3   OLD MAN: I like watching the children play. It makes me
4   feel young again. I was once, you know.

5   OLD WOMAN: I'll bet you were.

6   OLD MAN: So what do you like to do?

7   OLD WOMAN: Sit on this particular park bench and quietly
8   knit.

9   OLD MAN: *(Ironically)* Sounds really exciting, especially if
10   you drop a stitch or run out of that yarn of yours.

11   OLD WOMAN: Bet you'll never run out of yours.

12   OLD MAN: Huh?

13   OLD WOMAN: It was a joke.

14   OLD MAN: Hey, you like jokes, too?

15   OLD WOMAN: Yes. *(Thinks back)* My boyfriend had such a
16   wonderful sense of humor.

17   OLD MAN: My girlfriend loved mine. But that was a long,
18   long time ago. Must be nearly fifty years.

19   OLD WOMAN: A long time ago. *(Long pause, then)*

20   OLD MAN: Just what are you knitting there? An overcoat?

21   OLD WOMAN: It's a sweater for the winter. The landlord in
22   my building never turns the heat up above fifty-eight
23   degrees in winter. It's almost freezing. I can't take the
24   cold anymore. And to think I used to love skiing.

25   OLD MAN: My girlfriend liked skiing, but I never did.

26   OLD WOMAN: Sounds like my boyfriend. Anyway my land-
27   lord is so cheap, we all freeze in the winter when he
28   lowers the heat.

29   OLD MAN: He can't do that. It's against the law. You should
30   report him.

31   OLD WOMAN: I would if I had a phone or somewhere else
32   to go. But finding an apartment on my fixed income in
33   this city is like finding a needle in a haystack. And my
34   eyes aren't what they used to be. So I freeze.

35   OLD MAN: I know what you mean. My place is the same.

1   Freezing in winter and stifling in summer. Let me tell
2   you, I am looking forward to that new ice age — at least
3   in July and August. *(He watches her knit.)* You do like to
4   knit, don't you.

5 OLD WOMAN: Yes. I've been doing it for years. It keeps my
6   mind occupied. There's not much else to do anymore.

7 OLD MAN: Yes. I was going to join one of those senior citizen
8   clubs. But it's too far away from my apartment.

9 OLD WOMAN: Take a bus.

10 OLD MAN: Who can afford a bus? I can hardly afford a new
11   umbrella. *(He pops his open and it's full of holes.)*

12 OLD WOMAN: Looks like that one has seen better days.

13 OLD MAN: Haven't we all. It's been through a couple of
14   hurricanes and its share of downpours. How about you?

15 OLD WOMAN: I've been through a few storms in my day.
16   But, for the most part, I'm OK . . . except for the arthritis
17   and the lumbago.

18 OLD MAN: Don't forget the cataracts, and the famous
19   osteoporosis. It's very popular these days. Drink plenty
20   of milk. That's what they say.

21 OLD WOMAN: Look, if I don't have it now, I don't think I'll
22   ever get it.

23 OLD MAN: You can never tell. Just drink the milk to be safe.
24   But then there is cholesterol.

25 OLD WOMAN: That too. Still, regardless of rain, snow, hail
26   or heat, I haven't lost my ability to knit.

27 OLD MAN: I can see that. You're pretty good at it. You win
28   any knitting speed races? *(He thinks back.)* I had a
29   girlfriend once who liked to knit. *(Thinks, glances at her,*
30   *then shakes his head.)* But that was a long time ago. *(Looking*
31   *around, then up)* You think it's going to rain? *(She looks up.)*
32   What do you think?

33 OLD WOMAN: *(Shrugs)* Who can tell these days? It could rain.
34   Then again, it might not rain.

35 OLD MAN: Correct. It could snow.

1   OLD WOMAN: Snow?

2   OLD MAN: We had snow once in April, so —

3   OLD WOMAN: That was then. This is now. Remember? The
4   world is tipped.

5   OLD MAN: How do your bones feel?

6   OLD WOMAN: *(A little annoyed)* I beg your pardon. How do
7   yours feel, bub?

8   OLD MAN: Mine are fine. I have excellent bones for an old
9   codger. *(Putting out his hand to shake)* Sorry if I offended
10   you. *(She ignores his hand, so he drops it.)* I meant no harm.
11   All I meant was does your arthritis give you action
12   weather bulletins? My bones tell me a lot of things. They
13   are getting so good, I can tell when a subway train is
14   passing beneath us in one of those subterranean tunnels.
15   *(Holds his funny bone)* Oooo, there goes the 12:45 from Times
16   Square.

17 OLD WOMAN: *(She laughs.)* You're funny.

18 OLD MAN: What is this? Are you laughing? You should be
19   knitting!

20 OLD WOMAN: Yes, I know. But you see, I had a boyfriend
21   like that once. He made these silly jokes. *(She thinks back.)*
22   But as you so aptly put it, that was so long ago.

23 OLD MAN: *(Looks around, then gets up and walks about the stage.)*
24   I do love this park. I don't care if it's summer, winter,
25   spring or fall. I still love it. Can you hear that? *(Sound of*
26   *a pigeon cooing)*

27 OLD WOMAN: *(Stops knitting and listens)* What is it now?

28 OLD MAN: Sorry. I didn't mean to annoy you while you were
29   knitting. But I was just listening to the myriad sounds
30   of this sultry summer day and what do I hear but that.
31   *(Sound of pigeon cooing)* Hear that robin? I wanted to point
32   it out to you, thinking that you'd like to hear it too.

33 OLD WOMAN: *(Going back to her knitting)* I've heard it all
34   before. And it was not a robin. It was a pigeon. Don't you
35   know the difference?

1　OLD MAN:　Er ... of course! Yes. I was just ... testing you.
2　　　　　　Hear that? *(Sound of a siren)* Now that is really something.
3　　　　　　That's an Emergency Medical Services ambulance off to
4　　　　　　the rescue but helplessly trapped by grid lock. Not quite
5　　　　　　as romantic as the sound of a robin or a pigeon, but still
6　　　　　　part of the vast mystery of life in the big city. Ah, New
7　　　　　　York. I love you. Like that siren?
8　OLD WOMAN:　Terrific. It's right up there with honking
9　　　　　　horns and screeching brakes.
10　OLD MAN:　Exactly. I love New York. How about you?
11　OLD WOMAN:　I prefer anywhere else, but primarily Florida,
12　　　　　　especially in winter. Actually it's not bad in summer
13　　　　　　either. It's very quiet. Not as many people around to
14　　　　　　annoy you while you're trying to knit.
15　OLD MAN:　You can knit all year round down there without
16　　　　　　a single interruption I'll bet.
17　OLD WOMAN:　Yes. It's so quiet. I do like *(Looking at him)*
18　　　　　　quiet.
19　OLD MAN:　And warmth in winter.
20　OLD WOMAN:　Yes. Your fingers never freeze up.
21　OLD MAN:　You have family down there? In Florida, I mean?
22　OLD WOMAN:　You certainly are a nosey old man.
23　OLD MAN:　It comes from living alone for so long. You tend
24　　　　　　to talk to anyone you meet. Anyone.
25　OLD WOMAN:　Yes. Anyone. I've noticed.
26　OLD MAN:　Anyone — even compulsive knitters. *(Slaps his*
27　　　　　　*knee)* Why I even talked to a punk rocker the other day.
28　　　　　　He had hair like a porcupine. And safety pins for earrings.
29　OLD WOMAN:　And what did you talk about?
30　OLD MAN:　About fashion. He was into dog collars. I told him
31　　　　　　I once had the very same dog collar.
32　OLD WOMAN:　You wore a dog collar? Are you telling me
33　　　　　　that you were — or are — a punk rocker?
34　OLD MAN:　No, no. I'm telling you I once had a dog. I used
35　　　　　　to enjoy talking to him. His name was Duke. He was like

1   **you. Seldom spoke. Then he died.**

2 **OLD WOMAN: I guess you talked him to death.** *(She shakes*

3   *her head.)* **I guess you will talk to anyone.**

4 **OLD MAN: Yes, even little old ladies in Central Park who**

5   **knit non-stop.**

6 **OLD WOMAN: I'm sorry if it bothers you that I knit, but it's**

7   **what I like to do. It's my thing, as the young people say.**

8   **Don't you have any hobbies?**

9 **OLD MAN: ** *(Sitting close to her, she moves away a bit)* **I tried**

10   **model boat building when I retired, but after my first**

11   **boat sunk, I threw in the towel.**

12 **OLD WOMAN: You certainly give up easy, don't you. At least**

13   **when it comes to boat building.**

14 **OLD MAN: Me? Give up easy? Do you know how long it takes**

15   **to build a model boat these days?**

16 **OLD WOMAN: I haven't the foggiest notion.**

17 **OLD MAN: Well, let's just say Noah had it easy. Furthermore,**

18   **his directions came straight from** *(Points to the sky)* **you-**

19   **know-who. But when the directions come from a model**

20   **boat kit company, you are in deep trouble.**

21 **OLD WOMAN: So how long did it take you to build? Forty**

22   **days and forty nights?**

23 **OLD MAN: I wish. Sixteen months, twenty-three days. Then**

24   **it sunk — in twenty-three seconds. Right over there in**

25   **the lake. That was the end of my model boat building**

26   **stage. You know what I do now for fun?**

27 **OLD WOMAN: ** *(Looks at him, then down at her knitting)* **Once**

28   **again, I'm almost afraid to ask.**

29 **OLD MAN: Almost, but not quite, huh?**

30 **OLD WOMAN: That's what I said.**

31 **OLD MAN: You're improving.**

32 **OLD WOMAN: So what do you do for fun?**

33 **OLD MAN: ** *(Gets up and walks around)* **I used to swim, play**

34   **tennis, golf, ice skate, and jog, but now I've settled for**

35   **long walks in the park.**

1   OLD WOMAN: *(Looking at her knitting)* **You convene with**
2   **nature.**
3   OLD MAN: **I guess you could say that. It gets pretty wild**
4   **around here at times. But I enjoy it.** *(Sits beside her, and*
5   *again she moves away a bit.)* **You keep moving in that**
6   **direction, and you're going to end up sitting on the grass.**
7   *(She says nothing.)* **Just a friendly warning.** *(He twiddles his*
8   *thumbs and looks out over the audience.)* **Look at those**
9   **youngsters. Sitting side by side, or walking hand in hand.**
10   **There are even a few** *(Moves a bit closer to her)* **sitting really**
11   **close on the benches like us.**
12   OLD WOMAN: **Do you do this to all the women you meet in**
13   **the park. Or have you singled me out for particular**
14   **abuse?**
15   OLD MAN: *(Moves away from her)* **I just like to chat.** *(He sits*
16   *back, still watching the audience.)* **Isn't it romantic the way**
17   **they snuggle like that?**
18   OLD WOMAN: **I wouldn't know. My snuggling days are over.**
19   OLD MAN: **Not for me. And you shouldn't think that either.**
20   **You can never tell where your next snuggle will come**
21   **from.**
22   OLD WOMAN: *(Looking at him)* **I know where it won't come**
23   **from.**
24   OLD MAN: **Oh, I bet you'd jump at the opportunity. It could**
25   **be fun,** *(Looking away nostalgically)* **at least from what I**
26   **remember.**
27   OLD WOMAN: **I really don't care. And I would not jump at**
28   **the opportunity, as you put it. I just couldn't. What kind**
29   **of woman do you think I am? Those days are over for me.**
30   OLD MAN: *(Sadly)* **Yeah. I guess you're right.**
31   OLD WOMAN: *(Looking at him)* **Now that's a switch.**
32   OLD MAN: **What is?**
33   OLD WOMAN: **You're actually agreeing with me for once.**
34   OLD MAN: *(As if defeated)* **I know when I've met my match. I**
35   **give up. I surrender. I won't argue with you anymore. OK?**

```
1    OLD WOMAN:   Funny.
2    OLD MAN:   Oh, yeah? What is?
3    OLD WOMAN:   The way you said that. It sounded vaguely
4        familiar.
5    OLD MAN:   It's just age. It happens when you become senior
6        citizens.
7    OLD WOMAN:   Not to me it hasn't.
8    OLD MAN:   Maybe it's just me. Either everything seems
9        familiar, or nothing does. Anyway, to move on to another,
10       *less* controversial topic, where you from?
11   OLD WOMAN:   Originally? Or now?
12   OLD MAN:   *(Thinking)* Both. I'm from Greenwich Village now.
13       But I was born and raised in Queens. How about you?
14   OLD WOMAN:   *(Surprised)* Me, too.
15   OLD MAN:   You live in the Village?
16   OLD WOMAN:   No. I was born and raised in Queens.
17   OLD MAN:   A lot of us were. Those were the days. Remember
18       the trolley in Flushing?
19   OLD WOMAN:   I used to ride it to my Aunt's house. Remember
20       the hurricane of 1938? Talk about wind. That was a
21       whopper!
22   OLD MAN:   How could I forget that. My father had a summer
23       place down in Broad Channel, near the bay. We went
24       rowboating down Cross Bay Boulevard. That hurricane
25       caused some flood. It was great.
26   OLD WOMAN:   Yes, yes. I know what you mean.
27   OLD MAN:   *(He jumps up.)* Wanna play hide and seek?
28   OLD WOMAN:   Don't be silly. We are not children.
29   OLD MAN:   OK, OK. How about a video game? Space
30       Invaders, Dig Dug, or maybe Zaxxon! How are you with
31       a joy stick?
32   OLD WOMAN:   I beg your pardon.
33   OLD MAN:   You do know what a video game is, don't you?
34   OLD WOMAN:   Of course I do. It's ... it's a computer game.
35       Like Atari.
```

1 OLD MAN: Right. Only you have to insert a quarter. But
2   don't panic. I know you're on a fixed income. This'll be
3   my treat. So what do you say? You up for the challenge?
4   Hmmmm? Do you or don't you want to play a couple of
5   video games? I know a great place right outside the park.
6   They sell pizza. I'll even treat you to a slice of that. You
7   like sausage or anchovies?
8 OLD WOMAN: No thank you. There are too many people in
9   those places. Besides, I don't go out with strange men.
10 OLD MAN: I'm still strange, huh?
11 OLD WOMAN: No offense. But a girl has to be careful these
12   days.
13 OLD MAN: You have to take a chance once in a while.
14 OLD WOMAN: No thank you.
15 OLD MAN: You prefer being alone?
16 OLD WOMAN: I prefer the safety and stability of peace and
17   quiet and my knitting. Even when I was a teenager I liked
18   quiet places. I used to love going for a rowboat ride on
19   the Central Park Lake.
20 OLD MAN: So did we.
21 OLD WOMAN: We?
22 OLD MAN: My girlfriend and I.
23 OLD WOMAN: I guess a lot of couples do like to do that when
24   they're dating.
25 OLD MAN: How about we give it a shot. I'll do all the rowing.
26   You won't even have to sweat. Want to?
27 OLD WOMAN: No. No. I couldn't. Besides, we're not dating.
28 OLD MAN: And why not? Are you afraid?
29 OLD WOMAN: Me? No. I just *(Looks at him)* don't know you
30   well enough. You're very strange, you know.
31 OLD MAN: Oh, I get it. *(He sits beside her.)* You don't go
32   rowboating with strangers.
33 OLD WOMAN: Sorry. But I have my principles, my reasons.
34 OLD MAN: See if principles and reasons will keep you warm
35   on a cold winter's night when your landlord really lowers

1   your thermostat.

2   OLD WOMAN: That's why I'm knitting *(Holds up the sweater)*
3   this sweater.

4   OLD MAN: *(Not giving up)* **Do you jog?** *(She shakes her head no.)*
5   **Bike ride?** *(She shakes her head no.)* **So what do you do?**

6   OLD WOMAN: *(Holds up her knitting)* **I knit.**

7   OLD MAN: Yes, right. I forgot that. Listen, I'll treat you to
8   the boat ride if you'll come. How's that?

9   OLD WOMAN: I get seasick.

10 OLD MAN: Now that sounds familiar.

11 OLD WOMAN: I'm sorry if it sounds like an excuse. But a lot
12   of people get seasick. I also get carsick and airsick.

13 OLD MAN: So hang gliding is out too, I guess.

14 OLD WOMAN: Look. It has nothing to do with you.

15 OLD MAN: Then I'm not strange?

16 OLD WOMAN: I just don't want to get involved.

17 OLD MAN: Involved? We are just going for a boat ride. This
18   is not "Love Boat." It's summer fun for harmless old folks
19   in Central Park Lake. Come on. We're going.

20 OLD WOMAN: No we are not going. Please understand, I just
21   want to be alone.

22 OLD MAN: I felt that way once. But that was a long time ago.

23 OLD WOMAN: For me too. But it still hurts. That's the
24   trouble with men. They run off and never come back.

25 OLD MAN: Women aren't much better. I came back from the
26   war and discovered my girlfriend had left town. I never
27   saw her again. And we were supposed to get married
28   after I returned from the war. That's nearly fifty years
29   ago.

30 OLD WOMAN: I guess that happened to a lot of couples. The
31   boy meets a girl in France, Italy, Japan, or Germany or
32   the girl at home finds another boyfriend eventually while
33   her guy's away at war.

34 OLD MAN and OLD WOMAN: *(Together)* **Not me.** *(They look at*
35   *each other for a second.)* **Right.**

1	OLD MAN:	I guess I know how you feel. I'll never forget that
2		day. I got off the train after coming in from California
3		and took a cab right over to her house in Queens. And
4		what do you think I find?
5	OLD WOMAN:	I don't know. What did you find?
6	OLD MAN:	They've all up and moved. And she never told me
7		that in her letters.
8	OLD WOMAN:	That's funny.
9	OLD MAN:	Funny? It didn't seem funny at the time. I was
10		really hurt. How could she do that to me after all the
11		plans we had made for after the war.
12	OLD WOMAN:	No, I didn't mean it was funny that she
13		deserted you. I meant we, my mom and I, had to move
14		after my father died. I put it all in a long letter to my
15		boyfriend, who was overseas. But I never heard from him
16		again.
17	OLD MAN:	Maybe he never got the letter. Maybe it was the
18		mails. Everything was crazy during the war. Look at me.
19		Do you know how many letters I wrote to my girl that
20		never got to her. I was stationed in Japan after they
21		dropped the bomb.
22	OLD WOMAN:	Bombs. They dropped two of them.
23	OLD MAN:	Yes. Anyhow, I bet a lot of my letters never got
24		to her. At least not until everything was working again
25		over there in Tokyo. And how many of her letters never
26		got to me?
27	OLD WOMAN:	I guess on the battlefield some mail probably
28		was destroyed. And after the war some of it got lost. It
29		happened.
30	OLD MAN:	Right. Bombs were falling everywhere. And after
31		the bombs came the red tape. Who knows. Maybe she still
32		loved me, but her letters got lost and we just lost touch.
33	OLD WOMAN:	I know what you mean. My beau and I had
34		all sorts of plans. We were going to honeymoon in Niagara
35		Falls.

1	OLD MAN: We had planned to do that too. It was so popular
2	in those days before it was "better in the Bahamas".
3	OLD WOMAN: True. But as they say, the best laid plans.
4	OLD MAN: Yep. That's what they say.
5	OLD WOMAN: But he's gone, if not forgotten.
6	OLD MAN: I'll never forget her. She had this cute little
7	sailor's cap she used to wear. And she had this long blond
8	hair.
9	OLD WOMAN: She did?
10	OLD MAN: Yes. Why?
11	OLD WOMAN: Nothing. It's just that I had one of those caps.
12	OLD MAN: A lot of guys and girls did then. It was the war.
13	OLD WOMAN: You're right about that.
14	OLD MAN: What was your guy like?
15	OLD WOMAN: He was just funny. Like you. That's what I
16	remember the most, his sense of humor. I'll never forget
17	him no matter how long I live.
18	OLD MAN: Was he your first boyfriend?
19	OLD WOMAN: No. I was very popular. I was. I guess it's hard
20	to tell now. But I was the bee's knees once. So he wasn't
21	my first love. *(She looks down at her knitting.)* But he was
22	my last. He broke my heart when he never came back to
23	me after the war.
24	OLD MAN: So you've been alone ever since.
25	OLD WOMAN: Except for my knitting, as you know.
26	OLD MAN: I know. I know. *(He looks up.)* I guess I was wrong.
27	OLD WOMAN: About me?
28	OLD MAN: I meant the weather. *(He looks up and puts his hand*
29	*over his eyes to shade them from the sun.)* I thought it was
30	going to rain. But the sun is out brighter than ever.
31	OLD WOMAN: What about me?
32	OLD MAN: What about you?
33	OLD WOMAN: I do like to do other things besides knitting.
34	OLD MAN: You're kidding.
35	OLD WOMAN: No I'm not.

1   OLD MAN: *(All ears)* **Name one.**

2   OLD WOMAN: **I like playing the sax.**

3   OLD MAN: **The sax? You mean the saxophone?**

4   OLD WOMAN: **Yes.**

5   OLD MAN: **You're kidding. You? The knitter?**

6   OLD WOMAN: **Sure. I'm musically inclined, they tell me.**

7   OLD MAN: **I'd love to hear you play sometime. Anytime.**

8   OLD WOMAN: **Really?**

9   OLD MAN: **Sure. I love good music.**

10   OLD WOMAN: **How about now?**

11   OLD MAN: **Sure.**

12   OLD WOMAN: *(Puts her knitting down and pulls her saxophone*
13   *out of its case.)* **You ready?**

14   OLD MAN: *(Surprised)* **I don't believe this. Sure. What are you**
15   **going to play?**

16   OLD WOMAN: **How does this sound?** *(She plays a solo number,*
17   *then)* **You like it?**

18   OLD MAN: **That was terrific. My girlfriend, the one I lost**
19   **touch with, used to play the accordion.**

20   OLD WOMAN: **Me too. Isn't that a coincidence? But the sax**
21   **is sexier. The accordion was so square.**

22   OLD MAN: **I guess. So what other secrets to you have?**

23   OLD WOMAN: **None. How about you? You look like a man**
24   **of mystery.**

25   OLD MAN: *(Pointing to himself)* **Me? No, I'm just a lonely old**
26   **guy who likes to talk to a pretty lady when he sees one.**
27   **And you sure are one.**

28   OLD WOMAN: **You're only saying that because you like the**
29   **way I play the sax. Men go bonkers when they see a girl**
30   **playing the sax.** *(She winks at him.)* **Right?**

31   OLD MAN: *(Now he moves a bit away from her.)* **Huh? Well . . .**

32   OLD WOMAN: **Come on. It drives you nuts.**

33   OLD MAN: **Well . . . yeah — but I said you were pretty for**
34   **other reasons.**

35   OLD WOMAN: **Other resaons? What other reasons?**

1   **OLD MAN:**   Because you're just so nice to talk with. At least
2   now that you've put your knitting down.
3   **OLD WOMAN:**   Is that the only reason?
4   **OLD MAN:**   Well, to be honest . . . and I know this is going to
5   sound really ridiculous, but you remind me of her.
6   **OLD WOMAN:**   Your girlfriend from before the war?
7   **OLD MAN:**   Yes. Silly, huh?
8   **OLD WOMAN:**   No. *(She puts her saxophone away.)* **Not at all. In**
9   **fact, you're not going to believe this, but you remind me**
10   **of my guy. Funny, isn't it? I guess we're just two lonely**
11   **old people looking for someone . . . and, I guess, it would**
12   **be nice if that person was our long lost love.**
13   **OLD MAN:**   You're probably right. I know I'll never forget her.
14   **OLD WOMAN:**   And I'll never forget him.
15   **OLD MAN:**   *(Reaching into his pocket, he takes out his wallet and*
16   *removes a crumpled old photo and hands it to her.)* **Here's her**
17   **picture.** *(He stands up and walks around as she stares at the*
18   *picture. She begins to cry.)*
19   **OLD WOMAN:**   *(Turns to look at him)* **Billy?**
20   **OLD MAN:**   *(Turns and looks at her)* **How did you know my**
21   **name?**
22   **OLD WOMAN:**   *(She stands and they walk closer to each other.)*
23   **This is a picture of me.**
24   **OLD MAN:**   **Jenny?** *(She nods.)* **Is it . . . really . . . you?**
25   **OLD WOMAN:**   Yes, yes. Billy, it's me.
26   **OLD MAN:**   I thought I lost you.
27   **OLD WOMAN:**   I thought I lost you. *(They stare at each other for*
28   *a few seconds then fall into each others arms as the curtain falls*
29   *and the sax solo plays again.)*
30
31
32
33
34
35

The No-Fault Driving School

PRODUCTION NOTES

CHARACTERS: 1 male; 1 female.

PLAYING TIME: About 30 minutes.

PROPERTIES: Chamois rag, adult tricycle, road map, note pad, crash helmet, goggles, driving gloves, coins.

COSTUMES: MS. WHITE has on a white jump suit. ROGER has on white shirt, bow tie, plaid slacks, and black shoes and socks.

SOUND EFFECTS: Screeching brakes and tires, blaring car horns and air horns from trucks, loud rock music, sound of motor sputtering, Beach Boys "Little Duce Scoop" played very loud, traffic sounds, gears grinding.

LIGHTING EFFECTS: Daylight.

The No-Fault Driving School

3 **CHARACTERS:** MS. WHITE, the driving instructor; ROGER, the
4   student.

Scene 1

8 **TIME:** A summer's morning.
9 **SETTING:** Two chairs face the audience stage center. A slightly
10   battered sign hangs crookedly over an equally battered
11   building facade. The sign reads NO-FAULT DRIVING
12   SCHOOL. Then in smaller red letters under NO-FAULT
13   DRIVING SCHOOL are the words FOR THE SLIGHTLY
14   NERVOUS DRIVER.
15 **AT RISE:** MS. WHITE mimes polishing the car, which of course
16   is represented by the two chairs.

18 **MS. WHITE:** *(Polishing)* **Polish, polish, polish. My life has**
19 **become a chamois rag and a seat belt. I just hope Roger**
20 **has gained a little self-confidence since his last lesson.**
21 **He is not like the others. Talk about slightly nervous**
22 **drivers.** *(She shakes her head.)* **Roger is slightly terrified.**
23 **All I can say is if Roger is still anything like Mrs. Murphy,**
24 **I may need a** *loooooong* **rest. How can I forget Mrs.**
25 **Murphy? One-hundred years old and wanting motor**
26 **cycle lessons. Have you ever ridden on the back of a motor**
27 **cycle driven by a one-hundred-year-old hot rodder who**
28 **wants to do wheelies?** *(Stops and stands up straight)* **See?**
29 **It's happening already. I'm talking to myself.** *(She opens*
30 *the car door and sits down exhausted.)* **I've had it.** *(She rests*
31 *for a bit, curling up into a fetal position on the two chairs.*
32 *Suddenly she jumps up.)* **Did you hear that?! Brakes!**
33 **Twisted metal! Broken glass!** *(Holds her head)* **Calm! Calm!**
34 **Relax, girl. Easy. It was only a dream. Ha! It was more**
35 **like a nightmare.** *(Checks her watch)* **And it's barely nine**

a.m. Let's see. *(Pulls out her note pad)* **Let's see. Who do I have this morning. Please let it be anyone but Roger.** *(Turns pages, stops)* **Oh, no! It is him!** *(ROGER rides in on his tricycle and manages to fall over on it.)* **Roger!** *(She helps him up as she whispers to herself.)* **You're so clumsy.**

ROGER: *(As MS. WHITE helps him up)* **Hello, Ms. White.** *(Dusting himself off)* **I'm so clumsy, Ms. White. That's why Mom bought me this three-wheeler. I kept falling off my two-wheeler.**

MS. WHITE: **I know, Roger.**

ROGER: **Of course, I keep falling off my three-wheeler. But I'm hoping I'll do better with four wheels. What do you think, Ms. White? I'm so nervous.**

MS. WHITE: *(Dusting ROGER off)* **Still, nervous, huh?**

ROGER: **Terrified. I couldn't sleep at all last night.**

MS. WHITE: **I know what you mean, Roger.**

ROGER: **You do?**

MS. WHITE: **I do.**

ROGER: **You mean you're afraid of driving, too?**

MS. WHITE: **No, Roger. It's not exactly driving that's got me nervous. So, are we ready for our next lesson?**

ROGER: *(Takes a crash helmet, goggles, and driving gloves out of his knapsack. He puts them on.)* **I'm ready. What'll we try today? Releasing the emergency brake? Putting on our seat belts?**

MS. WHITE: **No, Roger. Today we will continue where we left off in lesson eighty-seven.**

ROGER: **Oh, yeah! I remember. Pre-driving techniques.**

MS. WHITE: **Right. Inserting the key into the ignition.**

ROGER: *(Wagging a finger at her)* **Ah-er, you forgot something, Ms. White.**

MS. WHITE: **To renew my life insurance?**

ROGER: **No, no. You forgot to buckle your seat belt.**

MS. WHITE: **Very good, Roger. Of course we do have to enter the vehicle first.**

1　　**ROGER:**　**Right.** *(Trying to determine how to enter the vehicle, he*
2　　　　　　*walks around "car", then is about to climb in over the back of*
3　　　　　　*the chairs.)*
4　　**MS. WHITE:**　**Roger, try the door.**
5　　**ROGER:**　**Door?**
6　　**MS. WHITE:**　**Yes, the door.** *(She mimes opening his door. He gets*
7　　　　　　*in. Then she goes over to the passenger's side and gets in.)* **What**
8　　　　　　**do we do now, Roger?**
9　　**ROGER:**　**Put both hands on the steering wheel and pray?**
10　　**MS. WHITE:**　**Cute, Roger. No. First we buckle our seat belts.**
11　　**ROGER:**　**Right! Buckle up for safety.** *(They do.)* **What's next?**
12　　**MS. WHITE:**　**Next we insert the key into the ignition.**
13　　**ROGER:**　**Ignition . . .** *(Looking for it)* **Ignition . . . Isn't that**
14　　　　　　**under the hood, Ms. White?**
15　　**MS. WHITE:**　**No, Roger. It's that little hole right there on the**
16　　　　　　**side of the steering wheel shaft.**
17　　**ROGER:**　**Ah-ha! I see it. Right next to the emergency**
18　　　　　　**blinkers — which I hope we'll never ever need. Do you**
19　　　　　　**think we'll ever need the emergency blinkers?**
20　　**MS. WHITE:**　**They're called flashers, and you can never tell.**
21　　**ROGER:**　**Well, I can hope.** *(He looks at "key hole" and mimes*
22　　　　　　*sticking key in.)* **There. I stuck it in.**
23　　**MS. WHITE:**　*(Getting impatient)* **Well . . . then turn the darn**
24　　　　　　**key and start her up, for pity sake!**
25　　**ROGER:**　*(Jumping)* **Yes! Right!** *(Turns key and we hear engine*
26　　　　　　*start up.)* **There. She's going.** *(Motor stalls out.)* **Oops. She**
27　　　　　　**stopped. Now what do I do?**
28　　**MS. WHITE:**　*(ROGER does these things frantically as MS. WHITE*
29　　　　　　*ticks them off. We hear grinding gears, motor sounds and*
30　　　　　　*sputters.)* **Release the safety brake, step on the floor brake,**
31　　　　　　**turn the key and press gently on the accelerator!**
32　　**ROGER:**　*(Out of breath)* **This is nerve wracking! There's so**
33　　　　　　**much to remember.**
34　　**MS. WHITE:**　**Don't panic, Roger. Eventually you'll catch on.**
35　　　　　　*(To herself)* **Or I'll burn out.**

1   ROGER: I think I'm going to panic!

2   MS. WHITE: Relax. Breathe deeply. Remember, this is only

3   your eighty-eighth lesson. There's plenty of time to panic

4   later, when we finally actually experience motion —

5   driving.

6   ROGER: How can you stand it?

7   MS. WHITE: Years of practice, practice, practice. How can

8   I forget? Now, as you remember, Roger, today we are

9   planning a cross-country lesson. Are you ready?

10   ROGER: *(Pulls out a crumpled up road map and gets tangled up in*

11   *it.)* Right, right. I brought my road map, just in case. We

12   won't get lost if I can help it. I was a boy scout — well,

13   almost. But we won't get lost. You'll see.

14   MS. WHITE: I hope we don't get lost, Roger. Last time we

15   wound up way out in the wilderness, and I was driving.

16   ROGER: But I was navigating.

17   MS. WHITE: Yeah. *(She shakes her head.)* By the stars.

18   ROGER: Well, they looked like stars. How was I supposed to

19   know they were landing lights of planes from the local

20   airport? Besides — *(Finally getting untangled from the map)*

21   It would have never happened if you hadn't fallen asleep.

22   MS. WHITE: I did not fall asleep!

23   ROGER: You did so. I heard you snoring.

24   MS. WHITE: Roger, I passed out when you panicked, pushed

25   me aside and jammed your foot on the accelerator instead

26   of the brake. Fortunately, by sheer luck, we did manage

27   to beat that one-hundred ton diesel locomotive across

28   the infamous deadman's crosssing. And the snoring was

29   my sinuses. Now, can we look at that map?

30   ROGER: Yes. *(He slaps it down, trying to flatten it out so they can*

31   *read it.)* Stay! There!

32   MS. WHITE: *(Jumps)* Ouch! Roger, you hit me.

33   ROGER: Sorry, Ms. White. I was just trying to flatten out the

34   road map so we could read it.

35   MS. WHITE: Well, don't. That hurt. *(Rubbing her knee, she looks*

1	*over the map.)* **Now let's see. We are here. And I think we'll**
2	**take the service road off Highway Forty-five up to the**
3	**expressway, and then take its service road out into the**
4	**boonies where there are only cows and no cars, so we**
5	**should be safe.**
6	ROGER: **Ahhhh, when are you going to let me drive on the**
7	**highway and the expressway?**
8	MS. WHITE: **As soon as you know how to distinguish your**
9	**left from your right.** *(Mumbles)* **Not to mention go from**
10	**stop.**
11	ROGER: **I learned that last week.** *(Holds up his left hand)* **This**
12	**is my right hand, and** *(Holds up his right hand)* **and this is**
13	**my left hand. Right?**
14	MS. WHITE: **You're getting closer, but we'll wait a little**
15	**longer. So, we're all set. Put the map away, Roger, and**
16	**let's get going.**
17	ROGER: *(Fumbles, trying to refold the stubborn map)* **OK. Right.**
18	**I'm almost ready!** *(He fumbles with the map until MS. WHITE*
19	*gets so aggravated, she pulls it off him and tears it to shreds.)*
20	**Ms. White! That map cost me eighty-nine cents.**
21	MS. WHITE: *(Trying to calm herself, takes a breath and then)* **OK!**
22	**OK!** *(Reaches into her pocket and pulls out change)* **Here! Here's**
23	**your eight-nine cents! Now let's get going!**
24	ROGER: *(Jumping)* **Right! Errrr . . .** *(Looks around, puts out his*
25	*hand to check the wind velocity and direction, then)* **Do I step**
26	**on the accelerator gently — or** *(They both get jerked back*
27	*from the accelerator)* **hard!**
28	MS. WHITE: **GENTLY! Just a gentle, gradual pressure!**
29	*(Covers her eyes and ducks)* **Look out for that gasoline truck!**
30	**I don't want to die in a fiery crash!**
31	ROGER: *(Cuts the wheel hard left and they get jerked right)* **Missed**
32	**it!** *(He wipes his forehead.)* **Phew. We're still alive.**
33	MS. WHITE: *(Peeking out between her fingers)* **Terrific. You're**
34	**improving.** *(She looks down at the speedometer.)* **Roger, notice**
35	**your speedometer? See anything unusual?**

1   **ROGER:** *(Looks down at it)* **Yes. It's right next to those barf**
2   **bags you always bring along.**
3   **MS. WHITE:**   **Notice anything else unusual about it?**
4   **ROGER:** *(He bends down to stare at it.)* **Errrr . . .**
5   **MS. WHITE:** *(Sitting back in her seat. She is terrified.)* **ROGER!**
6   **DON'T TAKE YOUR EYES OFF THE ROAD!!!** *(Loud horn*
7   *blares at them.)*
8   **ROGER:** *(Sitting up)* **Sorry. Did I miss something?**
9   **MS. WHITE:**   **Fortunately, yes!** *(Pointing over her shoulder)* **That**
10   **bus.**
11   **ROGER:**   **Hey. All right. I am getting better at this. I hit the**
12   **last one — and I was standing still.**
13   **MS. WHITE:**   **I know. I know. You swung open the door and**
14   **he tore it off. Now, Roger, about that speedometer . . .**
15   **ROGER:** *(Looks at it)* **It's reading one-hundred five.**
16   **MS. WHITE:** *(Holding on for dear life)* **And . . .**
17   **ROGER:** *(Looks at it again)* **A half? We're doing one-hundred**
18   **five and one half miles per hour.** *(Staring at her)* **Is that**
19   **legal?**
20   **MS. WHITE:** *(About to pass out)* **Noooo.**
21   **ROGER:**   **I didn't think it was.** *(He jams on the brakes; we hear*
22   *them screech. MS. WHITE gets thrown forward.)* **There. That**
23   **better?**
24   **MS. WHITE:**   **Well, five miles per hour at the moment seems**
25   **a lot better, but you can take the car up to thirty-five.**
26   *(He's ready to floor it.)* **Slowly, Roger!** *Sloooowly.*
27   **ROGER:**   **Whatever you say, Ms. White. It's just that I can't**
28   **think straight or drive straight when I'm nervous.**
29   **MS. WHITE:**   **I've noticed. Anyway, Roger, before we actually**
30   **arrive in the country, I want to go over a few more driving**
31   **fundamentals with you.**
32   **ROGER:**   **I'm all ears.**
33   **MS. WHITE:**   **Terrific. First of all, there's parking.**
34   **ROGER:**   **Parking. Yes, yes. What you do when you arrive at**
35   **your destination.**

1 MS. WHITE: Exactly. But there's more.

2 ROGER: More? Uh-oh. I knew it sounded too easy.

3 MS. WHITE: Easy, Roger. After parking, there's making a
4 three-point turn, a U-turn, and hand signals. And let's
5 begin by going over each one of those today.

6 ROGER: OK, Ms. White. Fire away.

7 MS. WHITE: Notice that sixteen-wheeler approaching us
8 rapidly from the rear?

9 ROGER: You mean the one about to climb up on our rear
10 bumper?

11 MS. WHITE: *(In a panic)* Yes!

12 ROGER: Yep. I see him. What do you think he wants us to do?

13 MS. WHITE: Can you guess, Roger? *(Loud air horn honks at*
14 *them.)*

15 ROGER: *(Looking in his rear view mirror)* If you ask me, he
16 looks like he wants to pass.

17 MS. WHITE: And how can you tell that, Roger?

18 ROGER: Besides the fact that he's doing this at me, *(ROGER*
19 *mimes cutting his throat)* he looks extremely angry. And
20 then there's all that horn blowing.

21 MS. WHITE: Roger, you're learning the clues to successful
22 survival on the road.

23 ROGER: I knew I would eventually.

24 MS. WHITE: Correct. And now, for our immediate good
25 health, I suggest you ease over to your right a tiny bit,
26 *(Covers her eyes)* because you're over the double line on
27 your left! And signal for that sixteen-wheeler to pass!

28 ROGER: *(Sticks out his hand and waves the sixteen-wheeler on as*
29 *he yells)* Come on, come on, you big dummy! Pass me! I
30 dare ya! Come on! Come on! Make my day!

31 MS. WHITE: Roger, I think you've been watching too many
32 Clint Eastwood movies! And, unless you have a desire to
33 end up with every bone in your head broken, I suggest
34 you simply give a polite wave to that monster behind us.
35 Something on the order of *(She gives a little wave to go*

1   *ahead)* **this.**

2   **ROGER: Got ya.** *(He waves the truck on, but then yells.)* **Come**
3   **on, you turkey!**

4   **MS. WHITE: No, no! No yelling at four-hundred pound,**
5   **sixteen-wheel truck drivers! Unless you have major**
6   **medical that pays one-hundred percent for re-attaching**
7   **your head.**

8   **ROGER: I think I have that. Dad took it out for me when**
9   **Mom bought me that three-wheeler. There. He passed us.**
10   **Now what do we do?**

11   **MS. WHITE: I want you to try some parallel parking practice.**

12   **ROGER: Gosh. What if I'm off a bit?**

13   **MS. WHITE: A bit?? Oh, look.** *(Points up ahead)* **You see that**
14   **parking space up ahead? The one between those two beat**
15   **up cars?**

16   **ROGER: Yep, and you see that one up there on the right**
17   **between that Rolls Royce and that Mercedes.** *(Pulls hard*
18   *right, they get jerked left.)*

19   **MS. WHITE: No! Not that one!** *(Covers her eyes)* **Not there,**
20   **Roger!**

21   **ROGER: *(She ducks as brakes screech and ROGER tries to park.***
22   *They are jerked back and forth, left and right, until we hear a*
23   *crash.)* **Ooops. I think I tapped the Rolls.**

24   **MS. WHITE: Roger, why didn't you park between those two**
25   **wrecks up there?**

26   **ROGER: I was aiming for them, but I missed! Sorry, but I**
27   **am a little near-sighted with these goggles.**

28   **MS. WHITE: *(Trying not to scream)* Then why don't you take**
29   **them off Roger?**

30   **ROGER: Then I'll be a little far-sighted and won't be able to**
31   **see the nose in front of my face. That could be extremely**
32   **dangerous. I mean, what with my allergy to cars, I could**
33   **sneeze and BAMB!** *(MS. WHITE jumps.)* **It would be all**
34   **over — or rather we'd be all over the road.**

35   **MS. WHITE: Right. Do not take those goggles off.** *(She gets*

1	*out.)* **Let me just leave a note on this Rolls.** *(She mimes*
2	*writing out a note and putting it on the Rolls.)* **I sure am glad**
3	**we picked up that no-fault dummy driver insurance.** *(She*
4	*gets back into the car.)* **Ease out slowly into the flow of traffic,**
5	**Roger.**
6	ROGER: **Should I look where I'm going first?**
7	MS. WHITE: **You'd have a distinct advantage if you did.**
8	**Check all around you, then double check behind you.**
9	ROGER: *(Looks behind him, but steps on the accelerator and they*
10	*are jerked back as we hear another crash.)* **Ooops again. I think**
11	**I tapped the Mercedes.**
12	MS. WHITE: *(Taking out her pad, she mimes writing a note.)* **Never**
13	**fear, Rog. I barely put away my pad. I'll just write another**
14	**note and we'll be on our way.** *(She writes the note and steps*
15	*out of the "car" and mimes putting it on the Mercedes.)* **There.**
16	*(She gets back in car.)* **That should do it. Try it again, Roger.**
17	**And don't worry. We're perfectly safe. All the oncoming**
18	**traffic has stopped at a red light, so we can pull right**
19	**out — after you've checked just to be sure it's all clear.**
20	ROGER: *(Looks around)* **All clear.** *(He pulls out so fast they are*
21	*jerked back.)* **What next?**
22	MS. WHITE: **My very words. Next we are going to find a nice**
23	**quiet corner and try a U-turn. How's that sound?**
24	ROGER: **Terrifying, Ms. White, but why do they call it a U-**
25	**turn?**
26	MS. WHITE: *(She looks at him.)* **Roger, because it's shaped like**
27	**a "Q".**
28	ROGER: **You'd think they'd call it a Q-turn then. Driving is**
29	**so weird, you know, Ms. White?** *(He smiles, staring at her*
30	*too long.)*
31	MS. WHITE: *(Sits back and covers her head in panic)* **Look out,**
32	**Roger!**
33	ROGER: *(Looks at road up ahead, then swerves out of the way of*
34	*oncoming traffic.)* **Missed me! So why do they call it a U-**
35	**turn if it's shaped like a "Q"?**

1   MS. WHITE: Roger, I was just kidding you. The turn is
2   shaped like a U, so it's called a U-turn.
3   ROGER: Sounds logical to me. This corner looks like a good
4   place to try a U-turn.
5   MS. WHITE: Are you sure you're not missing anything,
6   Roger?
7   ROGER: Well, I missed that sixteen-wheeler and the bus.
8   MS. WHITE: I meant are you sure you can make a U-turn at
9   this intersection?
10 ROGER: Not until I try it. *(He's about to until she grabs the*
11   *steering wheel.)* What are you doing, Ms. White?
12 MS. WHITE: *(Pointing up ahead)* Don't you see that sign up
13   there?
14 ROGER: The one that says "Kangaroo Crossing"?
15 MS. WHITE: No, no. I mean the one that says "No U-turns"!
16 ROGER: Oh, that one. I get it. We can't make any U-turns at
17   this intersection because of the kangaroos.
18 MS. WHITE: *(Too tired to disagree)* Correct, correct. In that
19   case, let's drive on down the road, until we find an
20   intersection without a sign that says "No U-turns".
21 ROGER: What if it's a "Kangaroo Crossing"?
22 MS. WHITE: We'll let them cross first!
23 ROGER: OK. But how about a little music? *(He reaches over*
24   *and mimes turning on the radio. Suddenly loud rock music blares*
25   *out.)*
26 MS. WHITE: *(Holding her ears)* Shut that off!
27 ROGER: *(Smiling and yelling)* Did you say something, Ms.
28   White?
29 MS. WHITE: *(Pointing at the radio)* It's too loud! Turn it off!
30   *(Holding her ears)* Turn it off!!
31 ROGER: *(Turns off the radio)* What did you say? I couldn't hear
32   you with the radio playing.
33 MS. WHITE: *(Yelling)* I said — *(Realizing she is yelling, calms*
34   *down and lowers her voice)* turn it down.
35 ROGER: I turned it off. Should I turn it back on and then

1   turn it down?

2   MS. WHITE: No! Please. Don't do that.

3   ROGER: Hey, whatever you say, Ms White. You're the
4   teacher. So what's next? Stunt driving? Wheelies? Should
5   we jump a river like Burt Reynolds did in "Smokie and
6   the Bandit, Part III"?

7   MS. WHITE: I think we'll attempt a few U-turns first, Roger.
8   We'll save river jumping for last.

9   ROGER: Good. Because I wouldn't have the nerve anyway.

10   MS. WHITE: Getting back to U-turns, let's try one at this
11   intersection up ahead. Be sure to look to see it's all clear,
12   then give it a shot. Be careful of that mailbox and the
13   phone booth on those two corners.

14   ROGER: I'll try my best not to demolish them. But I make
15   no promises. *(He adjusts his goggles and puts both hands on*
16   *the wheel.)* Ready?

17   MS. WHITE: *(Bracing herself)* Whenever you are, Roger.

18   ROGER: Hold onto your hat! *(As MS. WHITE tries to stay seated,*
19   *ROGER spins the wheel this way and that, we hear tires screech,*
20   *brakes screech, glass shatter.)* Ooops, there goes the phone
21   booth. *(Then with a bang, they come to an abrupt stop.)*

22   MS. WHITE: And there goes the mailbox. A perfect score.
23   Excuse me while I write the phone company and the post
24   office a note.

25   ROGER: No problem. I'll turn on the radio while you're
26   writing. *(He does as MS. WHITE gets out and mimes writing*
27   *the notes. She mimes bending way down, putting them on the*
28   *imaginary phone booth and the mailbox.)*

29   MS. WHITE: *(Getting back in car, reaches over and snaps off the*
30   *radio)* Are we ready to try the U-turn again?

31   ROGER: Ready and raring to go! I think I may be getting
32   over my fear of cars. *(Checks speedometer)* We're going forty
33   now, and I'm not even nervous.

34   MS. WHITE: I was afraid you'd say that. OK. Just keep your
35   eyes open for a good intersection.

1 ROGER: *(Takes his hands off the wheel and straightens his goggles)*
2 **I'll be like a hawk. These are eagle eyes.**
3 MS. WHITE: *(She gets more and more terrified as she speaks.)*
4 **Roger.**
5 ROGER: *(Hands still off the wheel)* **Yes, Ms. White?**
6 MS. WHITE: **How fast are we going?**
7 ROGER: *(Checks speedometer)* **Now . . . about . . . forty-eight**
8 **miles per hour.**
9 MS. WHITE: **That's about seventy-five feet per second.**
10 ROGER: *(Hands still off wheel)* **Wow!**
11 MS. WHITE: **At that speed there is one important rule all**
12 **drivers must obey. Do you know what it is, Roger?**
13 ROGER: **Hummmm, can't be the seat belt. That's fastened.**
14 MS. WHITE: **No, that's not it, Roger. One more guess.**
15 ROGER: **Adjust your rear view mirror.** *(He mimes doing just*
16 *that.)*
17 MS. WHITE: *(Screams so loud, ROGER jumps)* **NO! You must**
18 **keep both hands on the wheel at all times!**
19 ROGER: *(He grabs the wheel as a loud horn blares past them.)*
20 **Right!** *(He veers left.)* **Just in time to miss that explosives**
21 **truck.**
22 MS. WHITE: **Yes. We're so lucky.**
23 ROGER: *(Points up ahead)* **Look, Ms. White!**
24 MS. WHITE: *(Covers her eyes)* **What? Not another explosives**
25 **truck.**
26 ROGER: **No. Just a good corner to try a U-turn.**
27 MS. WHITE: *(Peeking between her fingers)* **Yes. You're right. Not**
28 **a truck or car in sight.** *(She sits up straight.)* **All right, Roger,**
29 **try that U-turn.**
30 ROGER: **Yeah!** *(He spins the wheel rapidly and they both get*
31 *thrown out of the car as we hear tires screech.)* **Wow!** *(Seeing*
32 *they are on the ground)* **Oops. Are you all right, Ms. White?**
33 MS. WHITE: **Fine, Roger. Just a few broken nails and bruised**
34 **knees. Can you analyze that U-turn for me? What do you**
35 **think you did wrong, Roger?**

1   ROGER: Wow, that's a tricky one. I thought we had our seat
2   belts fastened, both of my hands were on the
3   wheel . . . er . . . gee, I'm stumped. I can't figure this one
4   out. What did I do wrong?
5   MS. WHITE: *(Gets up and dusts herself off)* **How fast were you**
6   going, Roger, when you attempted that U-turn?
7   ROGER: Forty-eight miles per hour. Remember? I had just
8   looked at the speedometer. Was I going too slow? Is that
9   it? Yeah! I was going too slow. I should have been going
10   more like fifty, right?
11   MS. WHITE: A little slower.
12   ROGER: *(Gets up and dusts himself off)* **Slower? Around thirty.**
13   MS. WHITE: *(Getting back in car)* **Still slower.**
14   ROGER: Not twenty miles per hour. *(Getting in car)*
15   MS. WHITE: Close, but no cigar.
16   ROGER: Ten miles per hour?
17   MS. WHITE: In your case, a slow crawl, like one mile per
18   hour.
19   ROGER: Gosh. I was off by forty-seven. Hey, we're lucky to
20   be alive! I could have splattered us all over the road. We
21   might have made the five o'clock news! It would have
22   ruined dinner for Mom and Dad.
23   MS. WHITE: I know it would have spoiled mine. But that's
24   in the past. It's now time to try our U-turn at one mile
25   per hour. *(Suddenly we hear horns beeping.)*
26   ROGER: What are they beeping at?
27   MS. WHITE: I think you. You are blocking the intersection.
28   ROGER: Oh. Right! *(He starts the car and spins the wheel left and*
29   *right, jerking them right and left.)* **We're off. Back on the**
30   open road again.
31   MS. WHITE: Terrific. Try that U-turn up ahead.
32   ROGER: OK. Here we come. *(He turns the wheel, and they sway*
33   *from side to side.)* **There. How was that?**
34   MS. WHITE: Didn't we hit anything?
35   ROGER: Nope. Not even an elderly pedestrian. Pretty good, huh?

1   MS. WHITE: Roger. You did it.

2   ROGER: And with both hands on the wheel, too.

3   MS. WHITE: I don't believe it.

4   ROGER: Well, it's true. So what's next? I'm all ears.

5   MS. WHITE: *(Looking at the gas gauge)* **Notice anything**
6   **unusual, Roger.** *(The motor begins to sputter.)* **Hmmmm?**

7   ROGER: *(Looks around)* **No. Nothing unusual out here. Just**
8   **cows and chickens and country air.** *(He takes a deep breath.)*

9   MS. WHITE: *(As they sputter to a stop)* **How about now?**

10 ROGER: **We've stopped.** *(Tries to start the car)* **She won't start.**

11 MS. WHITE: **Any idea why?**

12 ROGER: **Let's see. I have the key in the ignition and I'm**
13 **turning it. But the motor doesn't work.**

14 MS. WHITE: *Soooo,* **what does that tell you?**

15 ROGER: **We have a bad motor?**

16 MS. WHITE: **No. Try again, but this time look at the gas**
17 **gauge.**

18 ROGER: *(Looking at gas gauge)* **Ah-oh. It's on empty. We're out**
19 **of gas.**

20 MS. WHITE: **Bulls eye. But don't panic. We passed a gas**
21 **station just three farms back, so you walk back** *(Takes*
22 *imaginary can out of car and hands it to ROGER)* **and fill this**
23 **can with gas — no lead. OK?**

24 ROGER: **OK. I'll jog.**

25 MS. WHITE: **Good idea. Off you go.** *(He starts off in the wrong*
26 *direction.)* **No, Roger!** *(Points in opposite direction)* **That way!**

27 ROGER: *(Still jogging, turns and jogs off)* **Be back in a jiffy, Ms.**
28 **White.** *(He exits and we hear a loud crash.)*

29 MS. WHITE: **Roger! Are you all right?**

30 ROGER: *(From Offstage)* **Yes. I just tripped over the gas can.**
31 **I'll be right back.**

32 MS. WHITE: *(Pacing)* **Why did I ever become a driving**
33 **instructor? I could have taken a less stressful job like a**
34 **bomb defuser for the police force, or a lion tamer. But**
35 *noooo,* **not me. I had to be a driving instructor. Maybe**

1	I'll quit and join a circus. I bet I'd make a great tightrope
2	walker. *(She mimes this, walking across the stage.)* **Yeah.**
3	**Maybe I'll do that.** After all, the only danger there is a
4	fifty foot fall onto the concrete floor below. *(She sits in car*
5	*and checks her hair and eyes in rear-view mirror.)* **Look at**
6	**that. Gray hair already. And bags under my eyes. This**
7	**job is getting to me. But I'm no quitter! I hang in there.**
8	**Still a job in the circus would be fun. I could spend calm**
9	**collected afternoons sticking my head into a lion's mouth.**
10	**ROGER:** *(Jogs on stage)* **Here I am, Ms. White. Got the gas.**
11	**MS. WHITE: No lead?**
12	**ROGER: No lead?**
13	**MS. WHITE: You did get no lead?**
14	**ROGER: Oh, yes. Right. No lead. Just gas.**
15	**MS. WHITE: Good . . .Well, pour it in.**
16	**ROGER:** *(Goes to front of car)* **OK.** *(He gets ready to pour.)*
17	**MS. WHITE: Not that end! The other end!**
18	**ROGER: I was wondering why there wasn't a gas cap.** *(He*
19	*mimes taking off gas cap and pouring in the gas.)* **There. She's**
20	**all in.**
21	**MS. WHITE: Then let's go. It's getting late.**
22	**ROGER:** *(As they get in car)* **Well, what now?**
23	**MS. WHITE: Start the car.**
24	**ROGER: Good idea.** *(ROGER tries and tries.)* **Ah-oh. Something**
25	**is wrong.**
26	**MS. WHITE: We probably have some dirt in the fuel pump.**
27	**That's what happens when you run out of gas.**
28	**ROGER: Should I jog back and get a new fuel pump?**
29	**MS. WHITE: No. Just keep trying to start her up. Maybe we'll**
30	**get lucky and get her going before the battery conks out.**
31	**ROGER:** *(Trying to start the car)* **Sounds pretty sick.**
32	**MS. WHITE: Keep trying.**
33	**ROGER:** *(Trying it)* **Yeah. Right.** *(It starts.)* **There she goes!**
34	**MS. WHITE: Halleluiah!**
35	**ROGER: What should I try now?**

1   MS. WHITE: It's time for us to head back, so let's try a three-
2   point turn right here. Make sure it's all clear, then
3   execute it.
4   ROGER: *(Looking all around)* **All clear.** *(Tries to drive)* **The car**
5   **won't move.**
6   MS. WHITE: Try releasing the emergency brake.
7   ROGER: Right! *(He does.)* Nope. Still won't budge.
8   MS. WHITE: Roger, use your shift.
9   ROGER: Shift, shift. Right! What a dummy. You have to put
10   **the car into gear.** *(Does it as we hear gears grinding. MS.*
11   *WHITE winces.)* **There she goes.** *(He turns the wheel this way*
12   *and that as they sway from side to side.)* **How was that?**
13   MS. WHITE: Not bad. You neither hit anything or anyone.
14   You're improving, Roger.
15   ROGER: Should I try anything else, Ms. White?
16   MS. WHITE: Just get us home in one piece.
17   ROGER: Yes. Mom is waiting for us.
18   MS. WHITE: Yes, Mom is.
19   ROGER: So how'd I do?
20   MS. WHITE: I would say fifty or sixty more lessons and you'll
21   be fine.
22   ROGER: Mom will sure be happy to hear that. Then I can
23   start teaching people how to drive.
24   MS. WHITE: They say miracles do happen.
25   ROGER: Right. After all, I did buy this driving school for
26   both of us, Sis.
27   MS. WHITE: Roger, I told you never to call me Sis while
28   we're working. And, lord knows, teaching my baby
29   brother to drive is *working.* So don't call me Sis.
30   ROGER: Sorry, Sis — I mean, Ms. White. *(He turns on radio*
31   *and the Beach Boys "Little Duce Scoop" blares out as he smiles*
32   *and drives happily — and menacingly — along. MS. WHITE*
33   *slumps down in her seat, holding her ears as the curtain falls.)*
34
35

The Proposal

PRODUCTION NOTES

PLAYERS: 1 male; 1 female.

PLAYING TIME: About 10 minutes.

COSTUMES: CLARK wears jeans and a tweed jacket. NANCY wears jeans and summer blouse.

PROPERTIES: Purse, 2 ring boxes, 2 engagement rings.

LIGHTING EFFECTS: Spotlights can be directed at CLARK and NANCY and dimmed.

SOUND EFFECTS: Sound of owl.

The Proposal

CHARACTERS: CLARK; NANCY, Clark's childhood sweetheart.

Scene 1

TIME: A moonlit night.

SETTING: A quiet park in a quiet town. Perhaps the sound of an owl can be heard. Sign on left side of stage says EAST ENTRANCE. Sign on right side of stage says WEST ENTRANCE. There's a park bench Center Stage. Trees are painted on the backdrop with a full moon above them and glittering stars in black velvet sky.

AT RISE: CLARK and NANCY enter from opposite sides of the park. They don't see each other.

CLARK: *(Stands by WEST ENTRANCE as a spotlight comes up on him. He checks his watch.)* **Where is Nancy? She's never late. Never. I told her I'd meet her right here by the west entrance to the park. Maybe she stopped for a container of coffee for us. She's always thinking of things like that.**

NANCY: *(Light dims on CLARK and comes up on NANCY as she checks her watch.)* **Where is he? Clark is never late. He hates it when anyone is late. Clark is the most punctual person I know.** *(She checks her watch again.)* **He should be here by now. He said he wanted to meet me right on this spot, by the east entrance at eight p.m., and it's now eight-twenty.** *(Light dims out.)*

NANCY AND CLARK: *(Spotlights come up on both of them as they check their watches.)* **Where are you? You're never late.**

NANCY: **Maybe he's had second thoughts like me.** *(Lights dim out.)*

CLARK: *(Light comes up on him.)* **I guess I'll wait a little longer and see if she shows up. I hope she does. I've been working on this proposal all day.** *(He gets on his knee.)* **Dear, sweet**

1	Nancy, I love you with all my heart. Too corny? Nah. Love
2	is never corny. Let's see . . . er . . . I love you with all my
3	heart. I've always loved you. Ever since we met in that
4	day-care center at age two, I've loved you. But . . . how
5	can I tell her? *(He paces around.)* I really don't want to get
6	married just yet. I know, I know. We promised to tie the
7	knot right after we graduated from college, but . . . *(He*
8	paces.)* I'm not really ready yet. *(Light dims out as spotlight*
9	comes up on NANCY.)*
10	NANCY: Clark, Clark, Clark. Where are you? I simply cannot
11	believe that you're late. I'll wait another minute, then I'll
12	take a walk over to our bench. I hope you're there waiting
13	for me because I've been waiting all day to propose. I
14	don't care what anyone says or thinks. I'm going to
15	propose to you . . . I guess. After all, this is the modern
16	world and I'm a modern woman. I go for what I want —
17	and I want you, Clark. I want you, Clark! You hear me?
18	I have ever since we met in that day-care center. We were
19	both two and loved to fight over the blocks and tinker
20	toys. So I'm going to propose. I've been working on it all
21	day. So far I've got, dear, sweet Clark, I love you more
22	than I love the sun or the moon or the stars. I don't know.
23	Sounds so really corny. But maybe it'll sound better when
24	I'm saying it to Clark. *(She paces.)* Why am I so unsure of
25	this? I want to marry him. I do love him. But why am I
26	so unsure? We promised to get married right after college.
27	And we graduated yesterday. So . . . so what do I tell him?
28	Yes? No? I don't know. All I know is I love him. *(Light dims*
29	out on her and comes up on CLARK.)*
30	CLARK: I guess she's not going to show up. Well, I guess I'll
31	take a walk over to our bench and look at the stars. Maybe
32	she'll be there waiting for me. *(Checks his watch as light*
33	dims out.)*
34	NANCY AND CLARK: *(Separate spotlights come up on them.)*
35	Times up. *(She walks over to the bench.)*

1	**CLARK:**	*(Checks his watch again)* **I'm off.** *(He heads for the bench.)*
2	**NANCY:**	*(As they see each other)* **Clark!**
3	**CLARK:**	**Nancy!** *(They run to each other and embrace.)*
4	**CLARK AND NANCY:**	*(Together)* **I thought you had forgotten**
5		**about our date. Who? Me? Never.**
6	**CLARK:**	**I was waiting for you by the west gate.**
7	**NANCY:**	**I was waiting for you by the east gate.**
8	**CLARK:**	**You were?**
9	**NANCY:**	**Yes. Just as we decided.**
10	**CLARK:**	**But I thought we had decided to meet by the west**
11		**entrance.**
12	**NANCY:**	*(She shrugs.)* **Oh, well ... I guess we just got our**
13		**wires crossed.**
14	**CLARK:**	**I guess so. Soooo ...**
15	**NANCY:**	**Soooo ...**
16	**CLARK:**	*(Looking up)* **Nice night, huh?**
17	**NANCY:**	**Oh, yes.** *(She looks up.)* **A full moon.** *(Owl hoots.)* **And**
18		**owls.**
19	**CLARK:**	**Yes. Very romantic.**
20	**NANCY:**	*(She looks up.)* **Look. Even with the full moon, you**
21		**can still see so many stars.**
22	**CLARK:**	**Yes.** *(Looking at her)* **Beautiful.**
23	**NANCY:**	**Yes. There's that same old bull again.**
24	**CLARK:**	**Huh? What bull?**
25	**NANCY:**	**The constellation. Taurus, the bull.**
26	**CLARK:**	**Oh! Right. That bull.**
27	**NANCY:**	**What bull did you think I meant?**
28	**CLARK:**	**Er ... I just thought you thought that something I**
29		**said was —**
30	**NANCY:**	**Bull?**
31	**CLARK:**	**Yes.**
32	**NANCY:**	**No, no.** *(She puts her arm on his shoulder.)* **Never.**
33	**CLARK:**	**Good. I'm glad.**
34	**NANCY:**	**Great. Soooo ...**
35	**CLARK:**	**Soooo ...**

1	NANCY:	How's . . . er . . . school?
2	CLARK:	I graduated.
3	NANCY:	You did?
4	CLARK:	Nancy? I did. Just like you. Yesterday. Remember?
5		You were there.
6	NANCY:	Yes, yes. Of course. Yesterday. No wonder it seems
7		like only yesterday.
8	CLARK:	Are you all right?
9	NANCY:	*(Pointing to herself)* Me? Yes. I'm fine. Why?
10	CLARK:	You seem miles away. Forgetting our graduation
11		and all. That's not like you.
12	NANCY:	No, no. I remember. It was very nice.
13	CLARK:	It was all right as college graduations go.
14	NANCY:	Yes. I'll say. *(Long pause)*
15	CLARK:	Nancy, is there something on your mind? You really
16		seem a bit preoccupied?
17	NANCY:	Is there something on my mind? *(She thinks.)* Er, no.
18		Anything on yours?
19	CLARK:	*(He thinks.)* Well . . . in a way there is. But it can wait.
20		Oh, by the way. I got that job with that company. You
21		remember. The one I told you about.
22	NANCY:	The computer job?
23	CLARK:	Exactly. I'll be starting as an assistant systems
24		analyst in their electronic data processing center.
25	NANCY:	That's great. I also got a job.
26	CLARK:	Terrific. Is it that assistant editor's job you wanted?
27		The one on the city paper?
28	NANCY:	Yep.
29	CLARK:	Great! We'll be working right across the street from
30		each other.
31	NANCY:	I know. We're pretty lucky.
32	CLARK:	I know.
33	NANCY:	So.
34	CLARK:	So . . . you going to take me to lunch?
35	NANCY:	Of course. I'll even take you to dinner.

1	CLARK:	How about breakfast? *(He winks at her.)*
2	NANCY:	We'll see. We'll see.
3	CLARK:	We will?
4	NANCY:	If you're good.
5	CLARK:	Good? I'm great.
6	NANCY:	Yeah. I know. Great.
7	CLARK:	When do you start?
8	NANCY:	Breakfast?
9	CLARK:	No. Your new job.
10	NANCY:	Monday morning.
11	CLARK:	Me, too.
12	NANCY:	Great.
13	CLARK:	Yep. *(Long pause)*
14	NANCY AND CLARK:	*(Together)* So, how was your day?
15	NANCY:	Oops. Sorry.
16	CLARK:	No problem. So how was your day?
17	NANCY:	Wonderful — if you like shopping for clothes for
18		work.
19	CLARK:	I know what you mean. It's a real pain. All the stores
20		are crowded. Parking stinks.
21	NANCY:	Yeah. I must have looked at two hundred dresses.
22	CLARK:	Buy a couple?
23	NANCY:	No. I didn't like any of them. I'll go shopping again
24		tomorrow.
25	CLARK:	Fortunately all I need is a suit.
26	NANCY:	Right. One blue, maybe one gray and you're all set.
27		Buy one?
28	CLARK:	No. Couldn't decide. It's not easy. Do you know how
29		many shades of blue and gray there are?
30	NANCY:	You have any idea how many styles of dresses there
31		are? And we women have to have a different dress on
32		every day. It's not fair. Or cheap.
33	CLARK:	But at least you'll be able to afford them with your
34		new job.
35	NANCY:	I know. I also want something else. *(She looks into*

1		*his eyes.)*
2	**CLARK:**	**Something else? Like what?**
3	**NANCY:**	**Can't you guess?**
4	**CLARK:**	*(He knows it's him. They sit on bench and he moves closer*
5		*to her.)* **Ummmm . . . you want a condominium?**
6	**NANCY:**	**No.**
7	**CLARK:**	**Not a condo. You want a . . .** *(Moves closer to her)*
8		**yacht?**
9	**NANCY:**	**No.**
10	**CLARK:**	**Hmmmm, what could you possibly want?**
11	**NANCY:**	**Don't you know?**
12	**CLARK:**	*(He stands up and walks around.)* **I guess I'm sort of**
13		**stumped.**
14	**NANCY:**	**Well, what do *you* want?** *(She walks over to him.)*
15	**CLARK:**	**A yacht *and* a condo.**
16	**NANCY:**	**Oh, yeah?** *(After a pause)* **Anything else?**
17	**CLARK:**	*(Scratches his head)* **What else is there? Oh! I know!**
18	**NANCY:**	**What?**
19	**CLARK:**	**A Mercedes 450 SL!**
20	**NANCY:**	*(Punches his shoulder)* **Clark? Is that all?**
21	**CLARK:**	**Is that all? Nancy, do you have any idea how much**
22		**a Mercedes 450 SL costs?**
23	**NANCY:**	**I really don't care, Clark. I have more important**
24		**things on my mind.**
25	**CLARK:**	**I know what you mean. I bet you're thinking about**
26		**how your first day at your new job is going to go and**
27		**whether or not you'll have enough pencils and paper.**
28	**NANCY:**	**Funny.**
29	**CLARK:**	**And whether or not you'll be near or far away from**
30		**the copy machine.**
31	**NANCY:**	**Very funny. Ha, ha.** *(Folds her arms and turns her back*
32		*on him)*
33	**CLARK:**	**Hey.** *(Turns her around)* **I'm only teasing you, Nanc.**
34		**You know me.**
35	**NANCY:**	**I know. But . . . well . . . I've been doing a lot of**

1 thinking lately.

2 CLARK: You have? About what?

3 NANCY: A lot of things. Mainly about us. *(She sits on bench.)*

4 CLARK: *(He sits beside her.)* I guess that makes two of us. *(She*
5 *drops her purse and he gets on his knees. He picks it up and*
6 *looks up at her, hesitating before trying to propose.)*

7 NANCY: *(She takes the purse from him.)* Thanks, Clark. *(She*
8 *watches him as he looks up at her.)* Were you going to say
9 something?

10 CLARK: Er . . . *(He gets up and sits on bench.)* No. I was just
11 thinking.

12 NANCY: Me, too. I've been thinking a lot lately.

13 CLARK: You have?

14 NANCY: Yes.

15 CLARK: About what?

16 NANCY: About *us*.

17 CLARK: Same here. *(He looks down at his knees.)*

18 NANCY: I love you, Clark. You know that I do.

19 CLARK: Same here, Nanc. I have —

20 NANCY AND CLARK: Since I was two years old and we met
21 at that day-care center.

22 CLARK: Remember how we used to fight over the blocks?

23 NANCY: And the tinker toys.

24 CLARK: How can I forget. *(After a pause)* So we both know
25 we love each other.

26 NANCY: How can I forget?

27 CLARK: And I haven't forgotten that promise we made
28 about —

29 NANCY: Getting married after graduation?

30 CLARK: *(Points at her)* That's the one.

31 NANCY: I remember. But, well, I . . .

32 CLARK: Yes? You what?

33 NANCY: I was thinking . . .

34 CLARK: I think we've both been doing a lot of that lately.

35 NANCY: We have. And . . .

1   **CLARK:** And . . .

2   **CLARK AND NANCY:** I think we should wait.

3   **NANCY:** Wait? About what?

4   **CLARK:** Errrr, you know.

5   **NANCY:** About the —

6   **CLARK AND NANCY:** Wedding?

7   **CLARK:** Yes.

8   **NANCY:** You think we should wait?

9   **CLARK:** At least until we see how our jobs work out.

10   **NANCY:** That's what I was thinking. *(She moves closer to him.)*

11   We'll still be best buddies?

12   **CLARK:** *(Putting his arm around her)* The best. Oh! *(Pulls away*

13   *from her)* I have something for you.

14   **NANCY:** You, too?

15   **CLARK:** What? You have something for me?

16   **NANCY:** Yes. *(She pulls ring box out of her purse as he pulls ring*

17   *box out of his pocket. She takes out ring, takes his finger and*

18   *slips ring on it.)* This is for my best friend.

19   **CLARK:** *(Takes her finger and slips ring on it)* And this is for

20   my best friend. *(They look at their rings then at each other.)*

21   **NANCY:** So how about I take ya to breakfast, buddy?

22   **CLARK:** If I can take you to dinner.

23   **NANCY:** No problem.

24   **CLARK:** Great. Boy, I'm glad that's settled.

25   **NANCY:** Me, too. Now, where did we leave off last night?

26   **CLARK:** I think . . . *(He puts his arms around her and he hugs*

27   *her as he speaks.)* I think my arm was here, and your arm

28   was here, and . . .

29   **NANCY:** Our lips?

30   **CLARK:** Our lips? Sort of like . . . here. *(They kiss as lights dim*

31   *out and curtain falls.)*

32

33

34

35

My Friend Never Said Goodbye

PRODUCTION NOTES

PLAYERS: 1 female; 1 male.

PLAYING TIME: About 10 minutes.

COSTUMES: ANNIE is in a dark summer dress. TOMMY is all in white.

PROPERTIES: Bouquet of daisies.

LIGHTING EFFECTS: None.

SOUND EFFECTS: Maybe sound of birds singing. But quiet other than that.

My Friend Never Said Goodbye

CHARACTERS: ANNIE: a teenager; TOMMY, Annie's friend.

Scene 1

TIME: Today.

SETTING: A park bench. Trees are behind the bench. It's a peaceful summer afternoon in the park. It's quiet except for the sound of birds singing. And it's not just a park. It's a cemetery. We don't see any tombstones, however. There is only one headstone, and it's hidden behind some weeds Up Right.

AT RISE: ANNIE enters, carrying a handful of flowers — daisies.

ANNIE: *(Stands by weeds, then sits on bench)* **I never thought anything like this could happen. Tommy, I thought you were my friend. Then you do this.** *(Pause)* **You didn't give anyone even a hint. You just ... did it.** *(She gets up and walks around.)* **Maybe if we had had a fight. Maybe if something had been bothering you.** *(She thinks.)* **Maybe something was. You were moody — but so was I.** *(She thinks.)* **Maybe it was my fault. Maybe it was something I did? Tommy?** *(She thinks; sit on bench.)* **Maybe. But it's too late now. You're gone. And I'll never know.** *(Looks up)* **Thanks, Tommy. Thanks for not trusting me enough to confide in me.** *(Pause)* **Tommy, we used to talk. We used to do everything together.** *(She tries to smile as she smells the flowers.)* **Everything.** *(She smiles and sighs.)* **It was always Tommy and Annie, never Tommy or Annie. We came as a set. Tommy, what went wrong? Was it me?** *(She pets the flowers.)* **This is not fair. You shouldn't have done it!** *(She is unable to speak.)* **I'm sorry. But you really know how to hurt a guy. You know? You hurt me. We had so much. We had something special.** *(She shakes her head.)* **"Had" is right. It's all gone now, but the memories.** *(She*

thinks, then smiles.) **You were always so shy. I'll never**
forget the first time you kissed me. *(She half giggles and*
sighs.) **It sure wasn't what I expected. I guess it wasn't**
what you expected either. It was . . .I'm not sure what it
was. But we managed to get it right that night. *(She is sad*
and mumbles the next two words.) **You rat. I miss that.**
Tommy, I miss you. I miss us. It's just not fair. Why did
you do it? You should have told me something was wrong.
You know us. We could have worked it out. We worked
out so many things together. We were always doing that.
You helped me and I helped you. Together we could solve
any problem — or so I thought. I guess this one was a
beaut, huh? But then you never asked for help. Tommy,
the he-man. Always keeping his feelings inside. Never
telling anyone. Sometimes not even me. At least I know
that now. You should have told me. *(Thinks)* **I should have**
asked. See? It was me. I knew it. My fault. *(She gets up and*
paces.) **Tommy, I'm sorry. I should have known something**
was wrong, but I didn't. *(Thinks)* **Yet . . . remember the**
last time we kissed? I should have known then. Oh, I
know at first you'd never admit you liked kissing me. You
were so cool. But once we got to really know each other,
you never stopped telling me how much you loved me.
Not so much in words, but in other ways. *(Thinks)* **Then**
it stopped. At first I thought you had found someone else.
No. That wasn't it. I should have known something was
wrong when summer came and you didn't want to go to
the lake, our lake, with me anymore. You always liked
the lake. We'd spend hours and hours alone out
there . . . together. *(She sits on bench.)* **You really hurt me,**
you know. I miss us together at the lake. I miss us alone
at the lake, Tommy. Do you hear me? I miss all those
hours and hours alone with you . . . *(There is a long pause.)*
So what can we do about it now? Huh? Tell me. Can you
do that? Is that possible? *(She waits.)* **I guess not. It's gone**

1   forever. Boys. Hey, I've been hurt by boys before. You
2   weren't the first. *(She covers her mouth.)* But you hurt me
3   the most. You never even said goodbye! *(She's almost in*
4   *tears, then controls herself.)* Not even a last hug. Tommy,
5   this is not right. You can't just do things like that to
6   people who love you. It's not fair. It's not. I wouldn't do
7   that to you. I wouldn't do that to my dog. But not you.
8   Not Mr. Macho. How can you hurt me like this? *(She is*
9   *silent.)* You were such an actor. You had all the other guys
10   thinking you were such a big man. When we were with
11   the others, you'd act so cool. You'd try to make believe I
12   was just some girl who happened to be lucky enough to
13   have you. I was nothing special. Just another female. At
14   least that's what you wanted the other guys to think. Hey,
15   I understood. You had to maintain your macho image
16   with the guys. We girls are not so dumb, you know. But,
17   Tommy, when we were alone. *(She smiles.)* You had a way
18   of making me feel . . . like . . . you made me feel good. Like
19   I was the only happy girl in the world. I couldn't imagine
20   anyone being as happy as I was. Did I ever tell you that?
21   It sounds funny even now, but it wasn't then, when we
22   were together. You shouldn't have done this. *(TOMMY*
23   *enters and sits on the bench beside ANNIE.)*
24 **TOMMY:**   I'm really sorry, Annie. *(She doesn't answer.)* Annie?
25 **ANNIE:**   *(Totally ignoring TOMMY)* It was just not fair, do you
26   hear me?
27 **TOMMY:**   Annie, it wasn't you. Really.
28 **ANNIE:**   I'll never know now if it was me. If I hurt you.
29 **TOMMY:**   Oh, no. Annie, you were the best thing that ever
30   happened to me. You were. Annie?
31 **ANNIE:**   You used to tell me everything, I thought.
32 **TOMMY:**   I did tell you everything. At least at first.
33 **ANNIE:**   *(She gets up and walks around, clutching her flowers.)*
34   And I always told you everything. There were no secrets
35   between us. None.

1   **TOMMY:** I know.

2   **ANNIE:** If I was mad, you knew it.

3   **TOMMY:** *(Smiles)* **I know.**

4   **ANNIE:** Maybe I was a grouch at times...

5   **TOMMY:** Hey. Never.

6   **ANNIE:** *(To herself)* **Yes. I was. I know I was. And we'd argue**

7   **and fight.** *(She smells the flowers.)* **But we always made up,**

8   **Tommy.**

9   **TOMMY:** We sure did. I'll always remember that. One of my

10   good memories.

11   **ANNIE:** So why? Can you tell me?

12   **TOMMY:** *(Gets up and follows her around, but she doesn't ever look*

13   *at him. He tries to catch her eye, but can't.)* **I can tell you this**

14   **much... Annie? Can you hear me? It wasn't you.**

15   **ANNIE:** I know it was me. It was always me.

16   **TOMMY:** *(Trying to catch her eye)* **No. No. It wasn't! I loved you!**

17   **I always loved you! I'll always love you.**

18   **ANNIE:** You probably just got tired of my grouchiness.

19   **TOMMY:** No. Never. Hey, I was a grouch at times, myself.

20   Remember?

21   **ANNIE:** But you were no angel, Tommy.

22   **TOMMY:** *(Sits on bench)* **Tell me about it.**

23   **ANNIE:** *(Covers her mouth for a second)* **Oh, I'm sorry.**

24   **TOMMY:** Hey. Stop apologizing. I'm not worth it.

25   **ANNIE:** See? Even now I hurt you. You never thought much

26   about yourself, and when I called you names you must

27   have really been hurt.

28   **TOMMY:** Yeah, I was — but I deserved it, Annie.

29   **ANNIE:** You'd always say, "But I deserved it, Annie." *(Pause*

30   *as TOMMY nods)* **I miss you, Tommy. Do you know that?**

31   **TOMMY:** I do now. Yes, I do now.

32   **ANNIE:** No matter how much we fought or called each other

33   names, I still miss you. And you didn't even say goodbye.

34   People who love each other shouldn't do that.

35   **TOMMY:** I know.

1	ANNIE: You should have told me something was wrong. I'd
2	never have left you. I loved you.
3	TOMMY: I was going to write a note, but . . . I couldn't think
4	of what to say. What could I say? You know me? I was
5	never much with words.
6	ANNIE: You were never good with words.
7	TOMMY: Hey, I could barely spell.
8	ANNIE: And your spelling. You spelled "Love" *(Spelling)* L-U-V.
9	TOMMY: She remembers.
10	ANNIE: How could I forget that? You were never good with
11	words. You had other ways of showing me you loved me.
12	TOMMY: Now that is one thing I'll really miss.
13	ANNIE: Big macho man. You'd die if the guys knew how you
14	used to pick me daisies at the lake and put them in my
15	hair . . .
16	TOMMY: Annie, don't . . . *(He's in real pain.)*
17	ANNIE: Who'd buy me silly cards and mail them to me for
18	no reason . . . but to . . .
19	TOMMY: Please don't, Annie . . .
20	ANNIE: For no reason, but because . . .
21	TOMMY: Don't.
22	ANNIE: Because you loved me.
23	TOMMY: *(It's as if he's been wounded.)* I loved you, Annie! I did.
24	Annie, please don't be sad.
25	ANNIE: Everyone keeps saying, "Annie, please don't be sad."
26	TOMMY: I'm not worth it, Annie.
27	ANNIE: "He's not worth it, Annie."
28	TOMMY: Annie . .. please . . . Annie.
29	ANNIE: Annie, Annie, Annie. What do they know? *(She sits*
30	*beside him on the bench.)* What did anyone know? How can
31	they possibly know how I feel? You broke my heart.
32	TOMMY: Annie, I didn't know.
33	ANNIE: Tommy . . .
34	TOMMY: Yes . . .
35	ANNIE: Why did you do this to me, Tommy? Can you tell me?

1	TOMMY:	It had nothing to do with you! Can't you hear me?
2	ANNIE:	I know it was me.
3	TOMMY:	*(Screaming in pain)* NO! IT WAS NOT YOU!
4	ANNIE:	Yes.
5	TOMMY:	No, no. Can't you understand? It was not you,
6		Annie. I love you.
7	ANNIE:	He never really loved me.
8	TOMMY:	*(In real pain)* What?
9	ANNIE:	If you loved me, you'd have told me.
10	TOMMY:	I did love you! And it had nothing to do with you.
11		Nothing!
12	ANNIE:	Whatever it was, it had something to do with me.
13	TOMMY:	No.
14	ANNIE:	Yes. I guess we're all partially to blame ... That's
15		what everyone says.
16	TOMMY:	No.
17	ANNIE:	I know it's true. I'll never forgive myself.
18	TOMMY:	It's not your fault, Annie.
19	ANNIE:	Yes. It had something to do with me.
20	TOMMY:	No, no, no ...
21	ANNIE:	It had everything to do with us —
22	TOMMY:	How can you say that?
23	ANNIE:	— because we were friends. And friends help each
24		other no matter what it is that is bothering them. That's
25		what friends are for.
26	TOMMY:	Annie, I'm sorry. I should have told you.
27	ANNIE:	Tommy, no matter what it was, I would have
28		understood. You should have told me.
29	TOMMY:	Annie, I'll tell you now. Can you hear me? Annie?
30		Are you listening to me?
31	ANNIE:	We always listened to each other. Always.
32	TOMMY:	Always.
33	ANNIE:	But now it's too late.
34	TOMMY:	No.
35	ANNIE:	Yes. Too late. You're gone forever.

1	TOMMY: Annie, I'm right here. Beside you. Right on this
2	bench. Can't you see me?
3	ANNIE: I'll never see you again.
4	TOMMY: Annie, look! I'm right here!
5	ANNIE: If I could only feel your arms around me.
6	TOMMY: *(He hugs her, but she feels nothing.)* **Annie, I love you!**
7	ANNIE: *(She shivers.)* **What was that icy chill?**
8	TOMMY: Chill?
9	ANNIE: I must be getting a cold. *(She stands.)*
10	TOMMY: A chill? From me? I love you.
11	ANNIE: I'd tell you how much I loved you. But it's too late
12	for that now. I'll never know why you did it, Tommy.
13	TOMMY: Annie, neither will I!
14	ANNIE: It was so sudden.
15	TOMMY: It was a dumb, stupid mistake. I was just so down
16	over so many things. It seemed there was nothing left.
17	ANNIE: You could have gotten help. Everyone can.
18	TOMMY: I know that now.
19	ANNIE: It's too late now. I know you could have worked
20	things out. Even this. Together we could have.
21	TOMMY: Yes.
22	ANNIE: I guess for as long as I live, I'll always blame myself
23	for what happened.
24	TOMMY: Oh, no. Annie, I'll never be able to rest in peace if
25	you think that.
26	ANNIE: *(Goes over to headstone)* **Look at these weeds.** *(She gets*
27	*on her knees, puts flowers on ground and pulls weeds away little*
28	*by little, revealing the headstone of TOMMY's grave. She picks*
29	*up the flowers and lays them on the grave.)* **These are for you,**
30	**Tommy. Daisies.**
31	TOMMY: Annie, I love you.
32	ANNIE: I'm sorry if I caused you any pain. And I'm sorry if
33	I can't come to see you anymore . . .
34	TOMMY: What? No . . .
35	ANNIE: It's been a year now. A whole new summer is here.

1   It's beautiful. I wish we could enjoy it together. I wish I
2   could be with you, but my doctor says it's not healthy to
3   dwell on the past. So, Tommy, I've come for the last
4   time . . .
5   TOMMY: Oh, no . . . please, Annie, don't leave me.
6   ANNIE: I just had to come here one last time . . .
7   TOMMY: No . . .
8   ANNIE: I had to come just one more time just to say goodbye
9   to you . . . my dear, sweet friend . . . Tommy. *(She stands.)*
10   TOMMY: Annie, no. Don't go. I love you! Don't go!
11   ANNIE: I have to go. Goodbye, Tommy. *(She exits.)*
12   TOMMY: Noooo . . . Annie, please don't leave me alone.
13   **Annie!** *(Curtain falls as TOMMY puts his head in his hands.)*
14
15
16
17
18
19
20
21
22
23
24
25
26
27
28
29
30
31
32
33
34
35

The Cabbie from Calcutta

PRODUCTION NOTES

PLAYERS: 1 male; 1 female.

PLAYING TIME: About 10 minutes.

COSTUMES: RAGGI wears jeans and Bruce Springsteen T-shirt. MRS. HARTFORD has on a gown, lots of diamonds and jewels. She also wears a lot of make-up and a gray wig.

PROPERTIES: The WALL STREET JOURNAL, a quarter.

LIGHTING EFFECTS: None.

SOUND EFFECTS: Sound of screeching brakes, revving engine, honking horns, and traffic.

The Cabbie from Calcutta

CHARACTERS: RAGGI, a young cabbie from India; MRS. HARTFORD, a rich widow from Fifth Avenue.

Scene 1

TIME: Today.

SETTING: Four chairs facing audience form the front and rear seats of RAGGI's cab.

AT RISE: RAGGI sits reading The WALL STREET JOURNAL as he waits for a fare.

RAGGI: **Look at this. Once more Polaroid and IBM are up. This is up, that is up. Good, great America. The land of much wondrous opportunity. Raggi, the cabbie from Calcutta, will be a very, very rich man someday. I don't spend all my life driving this hick ... or is it hack? Well, whatever it is, it's a necessity for Raggi now. True, it is also one big pain in the buttock, but then so was riding that blinkin' water buffalo back in Bombay. At least here you get paid. There all I got was bites by that infernal beast.** *(Paging through paper)* **And does Raggi see any water buffalo stock in this wondrous paper of the great American dream? No. Thank the great lord Rama. But Raggi sees much stock in many interesting things. Many. My heavens! Look at Sony. Sony is truly no baloney.** *(Just then MRS. HARTFORD enters.)*

MRS. HARTFORD: *(She walks up to RAGGI's cab and peeks in.)* **Cabbie? Yoo-hoo. Hello.** *(Annoyed, she shouts)* **Cabbie!**

RAGGI: *(Jumps and puts down his paper quickly)* **Oh, yes, dear lady. That is my middle name.**

MRS. HARTFORD: **Cabbie is your middle name?**

RAGGI: **Well, actually my middle name, it is Gandhi, after the great one. But in America, dear lady, it is Cabbie.**

1   You can call me Fred, you can call me Red — but when
2   you need a cabbie, please, dear lady, call me anytime
3   cabbie.
4   MRS. HARTFORD: *(In a hurry, bored)* **Yes, yes. How nice.**
5   *(Shakes her head)* **Another alien. Good lord, the country is**
6   **full of them.**
7   RAGGI: You telling, Raggi. In India we have your basic
8   Indian. But not in America. Here one person can never
9   tell from where the other is coming or to where he or she
10   is going. It's a very curious place America, but very great.
11   I am proud to be an alien in this great, wondrous land
12   of America. God bless the Grand Canyon and Bruce
13   Springsteen, who I hear was born in the U.S.A.
14   MRS. HARTFORD: Yes, well some seem to think so. As for
15   me, I'd just like to get this trip over with as soon as
16   possible. Do you understand my meaning, cabbie?
17   RAGGI: Oh, yes. Very well, misses. Yes, dear lady. And where
18   can Raggi take you?
19   MRS. HARTFORD: I'm on my way to Wall Street —
20   RAGGI: Good golly! Ah! Yes! Oh, how wonderful. The great
21   Wall Street. *(Holds up paper)* It is all here in black and
22   write.
23   MRS. HARTFORD: That's black and white.
24   RAGGI: Oh, yes, to be sure. That, too. Is it not amazing how
25   IBM and Polaroid are always up? *(Holds up the paper)*
26   MRS. HARTFORD: Oh, good heavens, not another one.
27   RAGGI: *(As he starts up his cab, we hear sound of engine revving*
28   *up.)* Another what?
29   MRS. HARTFORD: Another dirt-poor alien overly impressed
30   by our capitalistic system.
31   RAGGI: Oh. Well, one is truly amazed by such things when
32   one's family and friends live on a very few rupees a year,
33   and who must eat — but who have no money to buy food.
34   Slow, fast, or microwaved. And, dear lady, as a result,
35   you don't want to know what we poor folk must eat.

1   It is not a pretty sight, I assure you.

2   MRS. HARTFORD: I'll bet.

3   RAGGI: This would be a good bet. Truly our daily bread, it
4   is not what you call your microwave gourmet variety.

5   MRS. HARTFORD: Yes, yes. Well, so you've picked yourself
6   up by the proverbial bootstraps and have come to
7   America for our microwave TV dinners and our *(Fans*
8   *herself)* non-air-conditioned taxi cabs? Is that it?

9   RAGGI: Oh, the air conditioner is on full bust, but it's as hot
10   as buzzards out there. New York is worse than Calcutta
11   in summer.

12   MRS. HARTFORD: I'll agree with you there. So you've come
13   to America to make your fortune? Is that part of your
14   great American dream? Besides the TV dinners.

15   RAGGI: That is, indeed, part of what you call it, my American
16   dream. But there is also McDonald's and the Great
17   Cornell.

18   MRS. HARTFORD: The Great Cornell? What Cornell is that?

19   RAGGI: Cornell Sanders.

20   MRS. HARTFORD: I should have guessed.

21   RAGGI: Finger lickin' good, you know. Yes, indeed. And in
22   two very pleasant styles — regular and crispy. Truly
23   remarkable. And one is also entitled to a creamy rich
24   mashed potato treat and one amazingly good biscuit. Is
25   this not truly amazing?

26   MRS. HARTFORD: If you're into fast food.

27   RAGGI: Oh, yes. In India there is only fast food.

28   MRS. HARTFORD: There is? Really?

29   RAGGI: Oh, truly. One must run very fast to catch it, or one
30   has no fast food. Here the Cornell catches it for you.

31   MRS. HARTFORD: How interesting. Are we almost there?
32   *(She mumbles the next words.)* I hope.

33   RAGGI: Look!

34   MRS. HARTFORD: *(Braces herself in a panic, thinking she's about*
35   *to be in a tremendous crash — we hear brakes screech and horns*

1   *blow)* **WHAT?**
2   RAGGI: **Foot-long dogs sold right in the street!**
3   MRS. HARTFORD: **Foot-long dogs? Oh, you mean the Sabret**
4   **stand there?**
5   RAGGI: **Yes, yes. They even have a truly wonderful umbrella**
6   **for the monsoons. In India we have many monsoons, but**
7   **no truly delicious foot-long sabret dogs with chili,**
8   **mustard, relish, sauerkraut and such wonderful**
9   **umbrellas.**
10   MRS. HARTFORD: **It's a darn shame.**
11   RAGGI: **Yes, yes. Did I tell you about my trip to see the lady?**
12   MRS. HARTFORD: **What lady is that?**
13   RAGGI: **The great lady. The statue.**
14   MRS. HARTFORD: **In the Metropolitan Museum of Art?**
15   RAGGI: **No, no. In the truly wonderful harbor of the great**
16   **metropolis. The lady Liberty.**
17   MRS. HARTFORD: **Oh, that lady.**
18   RAGGI: **Yes, that lady.** *(Long pause, then)* **So aren't you going**
19   **to ask me about my trip to see the lady?**
20   MRS. HARTFORD: **I wasn't planning to. But if you**
21   **insist . . . So how was your trip to see the lady, cabbie?**
22   RAGGI: **I'm glad you asked. and please call me Raggi.**
23   MRS. HARTFORD: **Ragoo?**
24   RAGGI: **No.** *Raggeeee.* *(Spells it)* **R-A-G-G-I. The good old boys**
25   **down at the garage, at the pepper mine —**
26   MRS. HARTFORD: **Salt mine.**
27   RAGGI: **Huh?**
28   MRS. HARTFORD: **You mean salt mine. It's salt mine, not**
29   **pepper mine.**
30   RAGGI: **It is?**
31   MRS. HARTFORD: **It is.**
32   RAGGI: **This English is a very big pain in the buttock.**
33   MRS. HARTFORD: **Butt.**
34   RAGGI: **But what?**
35   MRS. HARTFORD: **Butt.** *(Spells it)* **B-U-T-T. Butt. The idiom is**

1   not pain in the buttock, but rather pain in the butt.
2   Another bit of America's gift to the free world.
3 RAGGI: So that's what it is . . .
4 MRS. HARTFORD: That's what what is?
5 RAGGI: An idiom. I know many of America's great idioms.
6 MRS. HARTFORD: I know many of America's great idiots.
7 RAGGI: You do?
8 MRS. HARTFORD: You're darn tootin'.
9 RAGGI: *(Turns and points to her)* **Yes!**
10 MRS. HARTFORD: *(Bracing herself — as we hear brakes screech*
11   *and horns blow.)* **Look where you're going! You're not**
12   **driving an ox cart now!**
13 RAGGI: *(Looking at the road ahead, dodges a truck — loud screech*
14   *of brakes and horns)* **Hit the dock!**
15 MRS. HARTFORD: You mean hit the deck!
16 RAGGI: Deck, dock. Here one has a wondrous variety of
17   possible obstacles to hit. In India the only thing you hit
18   is a sacred cow or a water buffalo.
19 MRS. HARTFORD: Don't they have any cars?
20 RAGGI: Oh, yes. But in my little village outside of Calcutta
21   we have no cars, no roads. We barely have any villagers.
22   Fortunately we are very lucky to be in walking distance
23   of the great city.
24 MRS. HARTFORD: Just a few blocks out of town, are you?
25 RAGGI: No, walking distance.
26 MRS. HARTFORD: That's what I meant. Walking distance.
27   A few blocks.
28 RAGGI: Oh, no, dear lady. In India walking distance is any
29   distance one can walk and not get trampled by a sacred
30   cow or eaten by a man-eating tiger. I lived thirty-seven
31   miles out of town.
32 MRS. HARTFORD: Good heavens! What do you do if you run
33   out of milk in the middle of the night?
34 RAGGI: Yes, telling me about flit.
35 MRS. HARTFORD: Not flit, it. Tell me about *it.*

1	RAGGI: I'm telling you already. Hold your haunches. This
2	could be a real boomer.
3	MRS. HARTFORD: I think you mean it could be a real
4	bummer.
5	RAGGI: Truly.
6	MRS. HARTFORD: Very dangerous walking in the India
7	jungle at night for a container of milk, huh?
8	RAGGI: No. Very dangerous milking a sleeping water
9	buffalo.
10	MRS. HARTFORD: You're serious.
11	RAGGI: I'm joking, dear lady. But we manage.
12	MRS. HARTFORD: I guess. But to be perfectly honest, I am
13	not at all happy by all you foreigners coming to my
14	country to rip us off.
15	RAGGI: Raggi rips no one. I keep this cab clean, and not
16	even one lady has ever torn or ripped her famous,
17	fabulous Leggs or silky soft, sheer —
18	MRS. HARTFORD: That's not what I mean! I was not talking
19	about pantyhose!
20	RAGGI: You said Raggi rip off people.
21	MRS. HARTFORD: I meant cheat them! As in take their
22	money unfairly and illegally! Cheat!
23	RAGGI: *(A bit annoyed)* Cheat? Raggi never cheat a single
24	person. I am an honest man! My father was an honest
25	man and his father before him. We are good people. We
26	are not cheats.
27	MRS. HARTFORD: Then you're not much of an American.
28	Here it's dog eat dog.
29	RAGGI: In India it's man eat dog, occasionally lizard. Now
30	*that* is *very* fast food.
31	MRS. HARTFORD: I think I'm going to be sick.
32	RAGGI: If you have to eat dog, you'd be very sick.
33	MRS. HARTFORD: *Stop talking about food!*
34	RAGGI: OK. What do you want me to talk about? Perhaps
35	the future of pork belly options on Wall Street? Maybe

1   margin buying and selling? Securities and Muni Bonds
2   are good. Or, perhaps, we can rap right on about . . . my
3   favorite . . . insider trading scandals. Very shifty, you
4   Americans. You do that in Calcutta, they cut off more
5   than your credit.
6 MRS. HARTFORD: Look, Rummie or Ronnie, or whatever
7   your name is, just get me to Wall Street. OK?
8 RAGGI: It's Raggi. With two g's.
9 MRS. HARTFORD: *Just get me to Wall Street!*
10 RAGGI: In a gypsy!
11 MRS. HARTFORD: What? This is a gypsy cab?
12 RAGGI: No. A fast cab. You know: in a gypsy. Pronto.
13 MRS. HARTFORD: Good gracious! You mean in a *jiffy*, not
14   gypsy.
15 RAGGI: Oh. I see. A jiffy. Like peanut butter? Is Jiffy peanut
16   butter fast food?
17 MRS. HARTFORD: I have no idea.
18 RAGGI: It sounds like a fast food.
19 MRS. HARTFORD: You're kidding, of course. Tell me you're
20   kidding.
21 RAGGI: Of course.
22 MRS. HARTFORD: Another bit of Indian humor?
23 RAGGI: Another bit of Raggi's humor.
24 MRS. HARTFORD: So Raggi, how does an immigrant from
25   Calcutta make his fortune in the Big Apple?
26 RAGGI: One works his B-U-T-T off. It is no picnic this Big
27   Apple.
28 MRS. HARTFORD: I'm sure. Do you plan the cabbie business
29   as your life's work?
30 RAGGI: No, no. I am enrolled at Columbia University. I am
31   some day becoming a system analyst.
32 MRS. HARTFORD: YOU . . . you mean you're a computer
33   programmer?
34 RAGGI: You bet! Yes. I am very well knowing of *Cobol,*
35   *Fortran, APL* and *Focus.* I'm even good at Space Invaders.

1   MRS. HARTFORD: I didn't even think they had computers
2   in India — let alone video games.
3   RAGGI: Of course we do. And here, too. I'm not going to be
4   driving this hick —
5   MRS. HARTFORD: Hick?
6   RAGGI: This cab.
7   MRS. HARTFORD: You mean hack — H-A-C-K.
8   RAGGI: I knew it. Hack. Anyhow, someday I'll be working
9   on Wall Street in the electronic data processing section
10   of Whitney, Wainwright, Wagner and Hartford.
11   MRS. HARTFORD: *My ex-husband's company?*
12   RAGGI: *(Ironic)* No?
13   MRS. HARTFORD: YES!
14   RAGGI: Imagine that. Only in America. Small world, huh?
15   MRS. HARTFORD: Too small.
16   RAGGI: They say it's a global village. Soon we'll all be one.
17   MRS. HARTFORD: How thrilling.
18   RAGGI: Yes. Soon I'll be raking in the big shmucks.
19   MRS. HARTFORD: I think you mean big bucks.
20   RAGGI: Yes, that, too.
21   MRS. HARTFORD: You couldn't do that in India?
22   RAGGI: In India a person of my cast can do only two things.
23   MRS. HARTFORD: And what are they?
24   RAGGI: Milk the water buffalo and feed the water buffalo.
25   It is a very limited job market with no IRA fund, no major
26   medical and absolutely no dental plan.
27   MRS. HARTFORD: Good heavens! What if you should get
28   kicked by a water buffalo? What do you do?
29   RAGGI: You kick him back.
30   MRS. HARTFORD: In America if you get kicked by a water
31   buffalo, you sue the owner and buy a condo in Beverly
32   Hills on the settlement.
33   RAGGI: Is this not truly the land of opportunity?
34   MRS. HARTFORD: Truly.
35   RAGGI: God bless America.

1 MRS. HARTFORD: Yes. I, too, love America. In my own way.

2 RAGGI: Well, here we are, dear lady.

3 MRS. HARTFORD: *(Getting out, hands RAGGI money and a*

4 *quarter tip)* **My fare, and here's a quarter tip for you.**

5 RAGGI: Truly God bless America. A whole two butts!

6 MRS. HARTFORD: That's two *bits*.

7 RAGGI: Right, no butt's about it.

8 MRS. HARTFORD: You mean you're not offended by such a

9 small tip?

10 RAGGI: Small? Listen, this is better than what you get for

11 driving a rajah on an elephant to Delhi.

12 MRS. HARTFORD: You're all right, Rags old boy. *(She exits.)*

13 RAGGI: *(Puts the quarter in his pocket, then opens the paper.)* **Now**

14 **let's see how many penny stocks I can buy for a quarter.**

15 **Good golly. That last penny stock I bought took a real**

16 **flying leap. Bought this cab company on that one.** *(Curtain*

17 *falls as RAGGI laughs and reads the WALL STREET*

18 *JOURNAL.)*

19

20

21

22

23

24

25

26

27

28

29

30

31

32

33

34

35

The Man in the Box

PRODUCTION NOTES

PLAYERS: 1 male; 1 female.

PLAYING TIME: About 10 minutes.

COSTUMES: MAN is dressed as mime, all in black with white face and gloves. WOMAN in casual dress: jeans and blouse.

PROPERTIES: Script.

LIGHTING EFFECTS: None.

SOUND EFFECTS: Loud gunshot.

The Man in the Box

CHARACTERS: The MAN; A WOMAN.

Scene 1

TIME: Anytime.

SETTING: An empty stage, painted entirely black. One chair, white.

AT RISE: The MAN stands Center Stage. He is miming feeling the walls of the box he is in. The WOMAN stands watching him.

WOMAN: *(Hands on her hips)* **I'm telling you there is nothing there. It's all in your imagination.**

MAN: *(Feeling walls of the box)* **What is? This stage? This theatre? This box?**

WOMAN: **There is no stage. There is no theatre. And there is no box! You just think there is. Now stop fooling around and let's go.**

MAN: **That's easy for you to say. You're not the mime. You're not the one on the stage, in the theatre, or stuck in this box.**

WOMAN: **Look. We've gone over and over this before.**

MAN: **Really?**

WOMAN: **Yes. Hundreds of times.**

MAN: **That many?**

WOMAN: **Yes. Now let's be reasonable. OK?**

MAN: **I'll try anything that will get me out of this play, out of this theatre, and, especially, out of this box — and back into the real world.**

WOMAN: **Great. OK. Will you trust me?**

MAN: **If it helps get me out of here. I'm willing to give it a shot.** *(He mimes shooting a gun and we hear a loud gunshot.)*

WOMAN: *(Holds her ears)* **What was that?**

MAN: **A gunshot.**

WOMAN: **It was not. It was just a sound effect.**

1	MAN:	Sounded pretty real to me. *(Sniffs air)* Smell that?
2	WOMAN:	*(Sniffing air)* What?
3	MAN:	Gunpowder.
4	MAN:	There is no smell of gunpowder! That was just an illusion.
5		This is just a stage and that was just a sound effect. I think
6		you're taking all this theatrical business too far.
7	MAN:	*(Points imaginary gun at her and she ducks.)* I aim for reality.
8	WOMAN:	I can see. Listen, will you let me try something to
9		get you out of there?
10	MAN:	As I said, I am more than willing to try anything if it
11		will get me out of here.
12	WOMAN:	Trust me. It will.
13	MAN:	You have my utmost trust. *(He stops feeling the walls of*
14		*the box for a moment.)*
15	WOMAN:	Terrific. I'll have you out of there in a jiffy.
16	MAN:	*(Loosening his imaginary tie and collar)* Great. Because
17		it's getting pretty stuffy in here. I knew I shouldn't have
18		worn a three-piece suit.
19	WOMAN:	What do you mean? You're wearing a leotard. And
20		this theatre is fully air-conditioned.
21	MAN:	Maybe the theatre out there where you are is, but it
22		is not air-conditioned in this box.
23	WOMAN:	*There is no box!* *(MAN backs away up against the rear*
24		*of his box, then calmer)* Sorry, sorry. Did I frighten you?
25	MAN:	You screamed so loud, you almost shattered the walls
26		of this thing.
27	WOMAN:	I did?
28	MAN:	Yes. You'll have to be more careful.
29	WOMAN:	Sorry. I'll try.
30	MAN:	Good. I'd appreciate it.
31	WOMAN:	So what are they made of? Glass? Crystal?
32	MAN:	What is what made of?
33	WOMAN:	The walls of your box. Are they made of glass? Or
34		is it crystal?
35	MAN:	I wish.

1   WOMAN: You don't know?

2   MAN: I haven't the foggiest. I'm not the writer or the prop
3   man, just the actor trapped in this thing. I don't build
4   them or create them. I just turn them into reality.

5   WOMAN: Maybe I should scream for help.

6   MAN: Be careful about screaming. OK?

7   WOMAN: I'll try, but you can be pretty obnoxious at times.

8   MAN: It's this box. It tends to do things like that to you.

9   WOMAN: It does?

10   MAN: It sure does. One day you're a totally free man, an
11   actor with a part to play, so to speak: you can go to the
12   supermarket, take in a movie, play tennis, go for a bike
13   ride — at least after the curtain has fallen; the next day —
14   wham! — you're a man trapped in a box. Don't ask me
15   why or how. But you're here. *(He feels walls of the box.)*

16   WOMAN: Don't you realize that you're just a mime?

17   MAN: I'm a man. And I'm trapped. And I'm running out of air.

18   WOMAN: I think you need a shrink.

19   MAN: I think I need a few air holes. Can you get a drill or
20   something and make a few air holes in this thing?

21   WOMAN: A drill? Wait a second. That gun you just fired.

22   MAN: Now you admit there was a gun?

23   WOMAN: I don't admit anything, but it seemed real enough
24   to you.

25   MAN: So?

26   WOMAN: So you must have put an air hole in your box when
27   you fired that gun.

28   MAN: Alas, no.

29   WOMAN: NO? Bullets make holes, don't they?

30   MAN: Yes, but it was a blank I fired.

31   WOMAN: Yes. I should have guessed.

32   MAN: Now about that drill.

33   WOMAN: Any particular kind?

34   MAN: No. As long as it's capable of drilling through this
35   thing. *(He bangs the walls with his hand.)*

1   WOMAN: Listen. Can we be reasonable?

2   MAN: You already asked me that and I said yes.

3   WOMAN: OK. Then why don't you just take two steps
4   forward and come over here and . . . kiss me?

5   MAN: Kiss you? *(He takes out a script and pages through it.)* **Is**
6   that in the script? I don't remember any kissing in the
7   script. Screaming I remember. There's a lot of screaming,
8   but —

9   WOMAN: *But no kissing!*

10   MAN: See?

11   WOMAN: *(Shouting)* See what?

12   MAN: Screaming. You screamed again. It's right here in
13   black and white. *(He imitates her line.) But no kissing!* See?

14   WOMAN: Yes, yes. All right. All right!

15   MAN: I told you. *(He puts script away.)* Would you like it better
16   if there were more — or at least some — kissing in the
17   script as opposed to screaming?

18   WOMAN: Yes, yes! I think I'd like that!

19   MAN: You would?

20   WOMAN: Yes. You are a good looking guy; I'm a woman. It's
21   what they call chemistry.

22   MAN: Is that what they call it?

23   WOMAN: Yes. It's what happens when two people are
24   attracted to each other.

25   MAN: Let me get this straight. You're telling me that when
26   two people are attracted to each other, they want to kiss?
27   And not scream?

28   WOMAN: Yes. They do. And maybe even scream a bit. It
29   depends.

30   MAN: On what?

31   WOMAN: On their chemistry. On how they feel about each
32   other.

33   MAN: I see. *(Feels walls of the box)* You know what I think?

34   WOMAN: What?

35   MAN: I think these walls have gotten thicker.

1   **WOMAN:**   *(Sitting down in frustration)* **Great.**

2   **MAN:**   **Great? It's terrible. Now I'm really trapped.**

3   **WOMAN:**   *(Standing, she's got an idea)* **Hold it! If the walls of**
4   **that thing are so thick, how come I can hear you and you**
5   **can hear me — perfectly clearly, I might add?**

6   **MAN:**   **What?**

7   **WOMAN:**   **I said — oh, now you're going to tell me you can't**
8   **hear me?**

9   **MAN:**   **Can you speak up? I can't hear you.**

10   **WOMAN:**   *(Throws her hands up)* **This is ridiculous.**

11   **MAN:**   **What?**

12   **WOMAN:**   *(Screaming)* ***I said, this is ridiculous!***

13   **MAN:**   **Great. I heard that. This sure is a predicament!**

14   **WOMAN:**   *(Not screaming)* **No, no. I said — oh, never mind.**

15   **MAN:**   **You're doing it again. Speak up. I can't hear you.**

16   **WOMAN:**   **So you won't come out of there even to kiss me?**

17   **MAN:**   **For some reason these walls keep getting thicker.**

18   **WOMAN:**   *(Paces)* **Right. OK. Forget I even mentioned a kiss**
19   **or love or taking a chance — or leaving that silly box of**
20   **yours. I think you're using it. Yeah.** *(Points at him)* **It's**
21   **your security blanket!**

22   **MAN:**   **I heard that! And, look, the walls are getting thinner**
23   **again.**

24   **WOMAN:**   **I think I'm beginning to see a pattern here.**

25   **MAN:**   **There. I can hear you again.**

26   **WOMAN:**   **Just as I thought.**

27   **MAN:**   **Thought what? That there's more to this than meets**
28   **the eye?**

29   **WOMAN:**   **Well . . .** *(Thinks)* **Never mind.**

30   **MAN:**   **OK. Do you want to come in?**

31   **WOMAN:**   **Can I?**

32   **MAN:**   **That's an excellent question. You know, no one has**
33   **ever tried.**

34   **WOMAN:**   **No one?**

35   **MAN:**   **I know. It's amazing. But in all my years in this box,**

1   I haven't been able to find a single woman willing to give
2   up her life outside the box, so to speak, to come and live
3   with me. Don't ask me why. But they simply haven't.
4   WOMAN: I wonder why not.
5   MAN: I have no idea. You'd think they'd like it in here. You
6   get regular meals, regular hours, regular days and nights,
7   regular pay.
8   WOMAN: Sounds pretty regular.
9   MAN: Regularity is what it is all about in here. There are no
10   surprises. It's all down in black and white. What do you
11   think? Sound like fun?
12   WOMAN: Does it to you?
13   MAN: Actually, it's not so much a matter of fun — or like or
14   dislike, for that matter.
15   WOMAN: It isn't?
16   MAN: Nope.
17   WOMAN: Then what is it?
18   MAN: It's more of a way of life. I can't remember when I
19   wasn't in this box. As far back as my most distant memory,
20   I was here — walled in by six planes of geometry. This,
21   alas, is my space. It's not a pleasant thought, but it's just
22   about the only one I have, give or take a few.
23   WOMAN: Wait a second. Are you now going to tell me that
24   you've always been in that box. I mean even before you
25   became an actor? Before you became a mime?
26   MAN: Even before I was born.
27   WOMAN: Before you were born?
28   MAN: As far back as I can remember.
29   WOMAN: Oh, yeah? Then how did you go to school?
30   MAN: In this box.
31   WOMAN: Sure. I guess it fit on the school bus?
32   MAN: Exactly. It's actually very portable. It goes where I go.
33   WOMAN: Really.
34   MAN: Of course. Watch. *(He walks to Left of stage.)* See? Now
35   I'm over here.

1   **WOMAN:** You're free!

2   **MAN:** Not quite. *(Feels the walls of the box)* **I'm still in the box.**

3   **It tends to linger.**

4   **WOMAN:** It's all in your head!

5   **MAN:** No. Actually, my head's all in the box. *I'm* all in the

6   box. Watch. *(He walks to other side of stage.)* See! Now I'm

7   over here and I'm still in the box. When it comes to

8   portability, I spell it *(Spells "box")* B-O-X.

9   **WOMAN:** But what about finding a girlfriend? Falling in

10   love? Getting married? Having kids?

11   **MAN:** What about it?

12   **WOMAN:** You can't do those things inside a box.

13   **MAN:** You do have a point there. It would seem a bit of a

14   problem. Kind of cramped.

15   **WOMAN:** Kind of cramped? A bit of a problem? It would be

16   a beaut of a problem.

17   **MAN:** Well, there are just some things in life I guess I'll have

18   to learn to live with — perhaps, to work out. Have you

19   ever thought of marrying a guy like me?

20   **WOMAN:** Who lives in a box?

21   **MAN:** Exactly. We could live happily ever after.

22   **WOMAN:** No, no, no. I could never marry someone who

23   thought his whole life was in that box.

24   **MAN:** It's not my whole life. I do have other interests, you

25   know.

26   **WOMAN:** *(Interested)* Oh, yeah? Like what?

27   **MAN:** I like to play box ball.

28   **WOMAN:** Very funny.

29   **MAN:** It's one of my box jokes.

30   **WOMAN:** That's it. I've had enough. I'm leaving.

31   **MAN:** You can't leave yet.

32   **WOMAN:** And why not?

33   **MAN:** *(Pulls out script)* Because you still have a page or more

34   of lines.

35   **WOMAN:** Oh, yeah? *(Grabs script from him)* Give me that!

1   **MAN:** *No! Wait!*
2   **WOMAN:** *(Tears up script as MAN mimes being torn apart)* **There!**
3   **Now what do you have to say?** *(MAN can't speak)* **Well! Cat**
4   **got your tongue? Say something.**
5   **MAN:** *(Picking up parts of script, reading a word here and there)*
6   **Love. Kiss. Scream.**
7   **WOMAN: Huh?**
8   **MAN:** *(Picking up more pieces of script)* **Wait! Scream. Life.**
9   **WOMAN: Hey, come on. It's over.**
10   **MAN: Hey. Come. Over.**
11   **WOMAN: That's it! I've had enough of actors! All they know**
12   **is the theatre. It's their whole life!** *(To MAN)* **I'm going to**
13   **marry an accountant!**
14   **MAN:** *(Reading last pieces of script)* **Accountant.**
15   **WOMAN: Good bye!** *(WOMAN exits.)*
16   **MAN:** *(Reads piece of script)* **Woman. Exits. The end. Curtains.**
17   *(MAN falls over dead as curtain falls.)*
18
19
20
21
22
23
24
25
26
27
28
29
30
31
32
33
34
35

PLAYS
FOR
MEN
ONLY

The Audition

PRODUCTION NOTES

PLAYERS: Cast can be either males or females. Two required.

PLAYING TIME: About 15 minutes.

COSTUMES: DIRECTOR wears casual business suit. CAT BURGLAR wears black shoes, black pants, black sweater, black ski mask.

PROPERTIES: File folders, scripts, black .44 magnum water pistol; bag with white dentist jacket, dentist mirror; telephone, small black duffel bag.

LIGHTING EFFECTS: Lights go out at end.

SOUND EFFECTS: Sound of telephone ringing. Loud sound of dental drill. Loud scream.

The Audition

CHARACTERS: CAT BURGLAR, actually the actor who is coming to audition; DIRECTOR.

Scene 1

TIME: Today.

SETTING: The office of a Hollywood movie director. There is an opened window Backstage Center with view of mountain with HOLLYWOOD sign on it. To the Right and Left of the window are movie posters of perhaps Bogart and Cagney in gangster movies. Below each poster is a filing cabinet. A desk sits Center Stage with a pile of scripts on each side. There is a telephone on the desk.

AT RISE: DIRECTOR, going through script, sits behind desk. Suddenly the phone rings.

DIRECTOR: *(Picks up phone, into phone)* **Hello? Ah, hey, babe.** *(DIRECTOR pauses for person on other end of line to speak.)* **Great, great. Hey, would I lie to you? No way. Yeah, I've been looking at this script. It looks good. Real good. Full of action. Yes. I have just the person in mind for the part of that crazy cat burglar. I know, I know. The title role is going to Clint or Bobbie. Hey, no problem. Don't worry. I really think I've found the right person for the part of the cat burglar. Right. No. Let me see how it goes. Yes, I will call you pronto. OK. Caio, baby.** *(DIRECTOR hangs up.)* **Look at this script! "The Psycho Cat Burglar Two." What a title. Action, shoot outs, car chases. Just what audiences love. I'll make millions on this one just like I made on "Psycho Cat Burglar One."** *(DIRECTOR gets up and walks to Front of stage. DIRECTOR pages through script as CAT BURGLAR enters quietly through open window. The CAT BURGLAR carries a small black duffel bag and what looks like a .44 magnum. CAT BURGLAR sneaks slowly up*

1   *behind DIRECTOR, who pages through the script. As CAT*
2   *BURGLAR silently climbs over desk)* **It's going to be another**
3   **box-office smash. We'll film the interiors in Hollywood, then**
4   **go to San Francisco and New York for the location shots.**
5   **CAT BURGLAR:** *(Sticks gun in DIRECTOR's back)* **Stick 'em up!**
6   **DIRECTOR:** *(Drops script and puts hands in air)* **Don't shoot!**
7   **CAT BURGLAR:** **Shut up!**
8   **DIRECTOR:** **My lips are sealed!**
9   **CAT BURGLAR:** *(Screams crazily)* **Shut up! Shut up! Or**
10   **I'll . . . I'll shoot!**
11   **DIRECTOR:** **Right! I'm totally silent!**
12   **CAT BURGLAR:** *(Acting very nervous, paces)* **Good. You scream,**
13   **and I'll . . . fill ya full of lead?**
14   **DIRECTOR:** **Huh?**
15   **CAT BURGLAR:** **That's movie talk. Right?**
16   **DIRECTOR:** **Right.**
17   **CAT BURGLAR:** *(CAT BURGLAR acts very nervous, hopping*
18   *around, pacing, waving the gun throughout the play.)* **OK.**
19   **Now . . . turn around real slow!**
20   **DIRECTOR:** *(Turning around very slowly, hands still in air)* **OK.**
21   **I'm turning now. Very slowly. Just don't shoot. I have a**
22   **family to support.**
23   **CAT BURGLAR:** **So do I.**
24   **DIRECTOR:** **Really?**
25   **CAT BURGLAR:** **Really. And these days it's not easy to feed**
26   **five hungry mouths.**
27   **DIRECTOR:** **You have five kids?**
28   **CAT BURGLAR:** **Kids? No. Dogs. Dobermans. They eat like lions.**
29   **DIRECTOR:** *(About to lower hands)* **I know what you mean.**
30   **CAT BURGLAR:** *(Pointing gun at DIRECTOR's nose nervously,*
31   *touching it)* **W-what are you doing?**
32   **DIRECTOR:** **Lowering my hands. Is that OK?**
33   **CAT BURGLAR:** *(Hopping around nervously)* **No, no, no! It's not**
34   **OK! It's bad! I hate that!**
35   **DIRECTOR:** *(Shooting hands back into air)* **OK! OK! Relax.**

1 CAT BURGLAR: Just don't make any funny moves, or it's —
2 *(Phone rings and CAT BURGLAR jumps.)* **W-what was that?**
3 DIRECTOR: **Just my phone. Can I get it?**
4 **CAT BURGLAR:**   *(Trying to decide as the phone rings)* **Er . . . oh . . .**
5 DIRECTOR: **I promise I won't say anything. OK?**
6 **CAT BURGLAR:**   *(Putting gun to DIRECTOR's head)* **Just one**
7   **wrong word and I . . . I —**
8 DIRECTOR: **Fill me full of lead.**
9 CAT BURGLAR: **Exactly. Not a word.** *(DIRECTOR nods.)* **You**
10   **sure?**
11 DIRECTOR: **Yes. I promise. Not a word.**
12 CAT BURGLAR: **Just remember, this is a .44 magnum. It can**
13   **shoot through trucks!**
14 DIRECTOR: **No problem. Mum's the word.** *(DIRECTOR walks*
15   *over to the phone and picks it up.)* **Hello?** *(At that, the CAT*
16   *BURGLAR pushes DIRECTOR aside and tears the phone out*
17   *of the wall and tosses it out the window then puts the gun to*
18   *DIRECTOR's head.)* **Easy. Easy. What did I do?**
19 CAT BURGLAR: *(Screaming)* ***You said hello!***
20 DIRECTOR: **Right. I just said hello.**
21 CAT BURGLAR: **Well. . . well . . . I don't like how you said it.**
22 DIRECTOR: **Oh, boy. I've got a loony in my office with a gun.**
23 CAT BURGLAR: **Shut up! And sit down!** *(DIRECTOR does, as*
24   *CAT BURGLAR kicks script out of the way.)*
25 DIRECTOR: **Hey, careful with that script. It's my only copy.**
26 CAT BURGLAR: **Oh, yeah? What's it for? One of those**
27   **crummy movies you keep making about nutty cat**
28   **burglars who use big guns to . . . to . . . you know.**
29 DIRECTOR: **How'd you guess?**
30 CAT BURGLAR: *(Really crazy now, pacing)* **I knew it! I knew**
31   **it! You make us all look bad!** *(Very crazy)* **W-we're not all**
32   **crazy maniacs, you know!**
33 DIRECTOR: **Oh, I'm sure! Hey, look at you.**
34 CAT BURGLAR: **Yeah? What about me?!**
35 DIRECTOR: **I bet you're a wonderful person.** *(Trying to lower*

1   *hands)* **Right? I bet you love to play Trivial Pursuit.**

2   **CAT BURGLAR:** *(Puts gun to DIRECTOR's nose)* **I hate that**

3   **stupid game! I always lose! And there you go again. I don't**

4   **like when you do that.**

5   **DIRECTOR: Do what?**

6   **CAT BURGLAR:** *(Screaming)* **Put those hands up! Fast!**

7   **DIRECTOR:** *(Putting hands in air real quick)* **OK! They're up! See?**

8   **CAT BURGLAR: Keep 'em that way.**

9   **DIRECTOR: I'll try. But they are getting tired.** *(CAT*

10   *BURGLAR puts gun to DIRECTOR's nose)* **Hey, I can keep**

11   **these hands up for ages. No problem.**

12   **CAT BURGLAR: I thought you'd say that. Just remember**

13   **this gun can —**

14   **DIRECTOR: Shoot through trucks?**

15   **CAT BURGLAR:** *(Looking around)* **Big trucks. I know it's**

16   **around here somewhere.**

17   **DIRECTOR: Can I help you? What are you looking for?**

18   **CAT BURGLAR:** *(Stopping to point the gun at the DIRECTOR.*

19   *Screams)* **HEY! Who gave you permission to talk? Huh? I**

20   **know I didn't. Now did I?** *(Pushes gun in nose of DIRECTOR)*

21   **Did I? Did I?**

22   **DIRECTOR: No.**

23   **CAT BURGLAR: I knew I didn't. Now . . . where is it?**

24   **DIRECTOR: Where is what?**

25   **CAT BURGLAR: You know! Don't act so dumb! You know**

26   **darn well where it is!**

27   **DIRECTOR: Money? I can give you money. I have lots of money!**

28   **CAT BURGLAR: Money? Really? Is that what you think I**

29   **want? Money?**

30   **DIRECTOR: It's not?**

31   **CAT BURGLAR: No! It's not! Boy, you're all alike. Money?**

32   **Now what would I do with money?**

33   **DIRECTOR: I . . . I just thought, you being a —**

34   **CAT BURGLAR:** *(Aiming the gun at him)* **Yeah . . .a what?**

35   **DIRECTOR: Well . . . you being . . . or having a gun —**

1	CAT BURGLAR: Oh! I get it! You were going to say me having
2	a gun and being a, quote "looney cat burglar," I'd want
3	money to buy bullets that shoot through trucks. Boy,
4	some people are really weird.
5	DIRECTOR: Hey, tell me about it. You meet them every day
6	out here in Hollywood. Like today —
7	CAT BURGLAR: You calling me weird? Huh? Just because
8	I like to dress in black and wear a ski mask? Is that
9	supposed to make me weird?
10	DIRECTOR: Hey. No way. You seem like a swell person to me.
11	CAT BURGLAR: *(Pacing around nervously)* Sure, sure. Because I
12	have this cannon. Did I tell you it can shoot through trucks?
13	DIRECTOR: As a matter of fact, you did.
14	CAT BURGLAR: Good. Because it can. And I love shooting
15	through trucks. Hey, I love my job. I love my dogs.
16	DIRECTOR: I love cats.
17	CAT BURGLAR: *(Screams)* CATS! I hate cats! They're all
18	weird! *(Pointing gun at DIRECTOR)* Right?
19	DIRECTOR: Yes! You're absolutely correct! Cats are weird!
20	CAT BURGLAR: See! I told you they were.
21	DIRECTOR: You're absolutely right. Listen, can I ask you a
22	favor?
23	CAT BURGLAR: A favor? Like what?
24	DIRECTOR: Well, my arms are really getting very tired. Can
25	I put them down?
26	CAT BURGLAR: Sure, but I'll . . . you know what.
27	DIRECTOR: Forget I even mentioned it. I'll keep them up.
28	CAT BURGLAR: Good idea. Wait!
29	DIRECTOR: *(Sits back in chair, ready to be blown away)* Don't shoot!
30	CAT BURGLAR: *(Reaching in pocket)* No, no. I just remembered. I
31	have these handcuffs I took off this . . . er . . . police person.
32	DIRECTOR: Y-you robbed a police officer?
33	CAT BURGLAR: *(Points gun at DIRECTOR's ear)* Who told you
34	that?
35	DIRECTOR: Y-you did.

1 CAT BURGLAR: Well . . . I lied! I got them at a . . . a magic
2 shop!
3 DIRECTOR: OK. I believe you. You got them at a magic shop.
4 A lot of people do that. Nearly everyone I know has a
5 pair of handcuffs that they bought at a magic shop.
6 CAT BURGLAR: You must know some really weird people.
7 DIRECTOR: Hey, it's Hollywood. That's show biz. Right?
8 CAT BURGLAR: Right. Put out your hands. *(DIRECTOR*
9 *does.)* **Here.** *(Gives handcuffs to DIRECTOR)* **Handcuff**
10 **yourself to that chair. And one false move and it's curtains.**
11 DIRECTOR: Curtains?
12 CAT BURGLAR: Yeah. Curtains. Isn't that what Cagney and
13 Bogart said in all their movies?
14 DIRECTOR: *(Handcuffing self to chair)* Right. Many times.
15 CAT BURGLAR: And don't you forget it. Cagney and Bogie
16 were real stars. They knew what it was like to be real
17 crazy, not like the wimps you put on the screen today.
18 DIRECTOR: I fully agree.
19 CAT BURGLAR: You're just saying that because you're
20 afraid I'll plug ya with my gat.
21 DIRECTOR: Gat?
22 CAT BURGLAR: Yeah. You know. Gat. Rod. Heater. That's
23 what Jimmie and Bogie used to call a gun.
24 DIRECTOR: Right. Yes. Of course. A gat.
25 CAR BURGLAR: *(Pacing nervously)* Yeah, right. So where is
26 it? Huh? Where'd you hide it?
27 DIRECTOR: Hide what?
28 CAT BURGLAR: You know what I mean! *(Goes to filing cabinet*
29 *Stage Left and begins pulling out papers, tossing them about.)*
30 Where is it? I know it's here somewhere! It's got to be!
31 DIRECTOR: If you'd just tell me what it is you're after, I'll
32 tell you where it is.
33 CAT BURGLAR: Oh, sure, sure. That . . . that would be too
34 easy.
35 DIRECTOR: Listen, I'd better warn you. I have someone

1   coming to audition for a part in my next movie —

2 CAT BURGLAR: Another one of those crazy cat burglar
3   pictures?

4 DIRECTOR: Well . . .

5 CAT BURGLAR: *(Hopping mad, waves gun wildly around,*
6   *screams)* **I knew it! I knew it! You make us all look like**
7   **crazy, wild, maniacs!** *I hate that!* *(Holds gun with both hands*
8   *and gets into firing position, aiming at DIRECTOR.)* **I ought —**

9 DIRECTOR: Oh, no! No! Don't do that! Please don't shoot!

10 CAT BURGLAR: Then shut up and tell me where it is!

11 DIRECTOR: Where is what?

12 CAT BURGLAR: *(Goes over to other filing cabinet and tosses the*
13   *scripts and papers all over, then screams)* **Where is it?! I know**
14   **it's around here somewhere. Where is it?!**

15 DIRECTOR: What? What?

16 CAT BURGLAR: **It!** *(Stops and grabs DIRECTOR's hair and puts*
17   *gun in DIRECTOR's mouth.)* **Oh, I get it! Trying to hold out**
18   **on me, eh? Is that it? Hmmmm? You know what I do to**
19   **rats who hold out on me?**

20 DIRECTOR: *(Mumbling with gun in mouth)* **Na-num.**

21 CAT BURGLAR: *(Pulling gun out of DIRECTOR's mouth)* **What?**

22 DIRECTOR: I said, no.

23 CAT BURGLAR: Well, I'll tell you what I do to rats who hold
24   out on me. *(Screaming)* **I air-condition 'em!**

25 DIRECTOR: Excellent idea.

26 CAT BURGLAR: *(Pointing gun in DIRECTOR's nose)* **It's only**
27   **fair. Right? Am I right? Or do you think I'm just crazy?**

28 DIRECTOR: Yes.

29 CAT BURGLAR: Yes, I'm crazy, or, yes, I'm right?

30 DIRECTOR: Yes, you're . . .

31 CAT BURGLAR: What?

32 DIRECTOR: You're right.

33 CAT BURGLAR: *(Pushing DIRECTOR out from behind desk)* **I**
34   **know that, you dummy!** *(CAT BURGLAR begins to throw*
35   *papers from the desk drawers around. Screams.)* **Where is it?**

1   Where is it?

2   DIRECTOR: Look, any minute that person is going to arrive

3   for that audition —

4   CAT BURGLAR: Yeah, so?

5   DIRECTOR: So I don't want anyone to get hurt.

6   CAT BURGLAR: You afraid of a little bloodshed?

7   DIRECTOR: I just don't want anyone to get shot. Including

8   you.

9   CAT BURGLAR: What is this actor? A copper? The rat got a

10   rod? Huh? Is that it?

11   DIRECTOR: No, no. But you might get nervous and shoot

12   someone.

13   CAT BURGLAR: Yep. I often do that.

14   DIRECTOR: Terrific.

15   CAT BURGLAR: Yep. I love my rod, my gat. It's man's best

16   friend — next to his dogs. Did I tell you I have dogs — and

17   I hate cats?

18   DIRECTOR: Yes. And you're right in hating them. Cats are

19   shifty little creeps that sneak up on you from behind just

20   like —

21   CAT BURGLAR: *(Pointing gun at him)* Like me? Is that what

22   you were going to say?

23   DIRECTOR: NO, NO! Really. I think you're . . . you're —

24   CAT BURGLAR: A nut? A mad cat burglar? *Bananas?!* Is that it?

25   DIRECTOR: Not at all. Hey, I happen to know that

26   underneath that . . . that —

27   CAT BURGLAR: Demented exterior?

28   DIRECTOR: No. I was going to say that underneath

29   those . . . black clothes and that . . . nifty-looking ski

30   mask, you're probably one of the nicest people you'd ever

31   want to meet. Right?

32   CAT BURGLAR: Nope.

33   DIRECTOR: N-no?

34   CAT BURGLAR: Nope. Actually I'm a crazy cat burglar.

35   DIRECTOR: Terrific.

1	CAT BURGLAR: No. It's not terrific. But it's what I do best.
2	Hey, it's a living. Right?
3	DIRECTOR: *(Not so sure)* I guess.
4	CAT BURGLAR: You don't sound so sure. *(Puts gun in*
5	*DIRECTOR's face)* Are you sure or aren't you?
6	DIRECTOR: I'm positive. Positive!
7	CAT BURGLAR: *(On the floor, tossing papers around)* Where is
8	it? Where is it?
9	DIRECTOR: I know! You're looking for jewels!
10	CAR BURGLAR: *(Getting up)* What?
11	DIRECTOR: Sure. All you cat burglars are after jewels, correct?
12	CAT BURGLAR: No. You're absolutely incorrect. *(Looking*
13	*through scripts on desk, tossing them around.)* I know it's here
14	somewhere.
15	DIRECTOR: *(Looking at watch)* Look. That person will be here
16	any minute now for that audition. You better just take
17	what you're looking for and get away while the getting
18	is good.
19	CAT BURGLAR: Very good. Are those lines from one of your
20	crummy scripts? One of those where the rogue cop points
21	his .44 magnum at the crazed cat burglar *(Points his gun*
22	*at DIRECTOR)* and says make my day? Is that it?
23	DIRECTOR: Well ...
24	CAT BURGLAR: *(Hopping around like a nut, jumps on desk, kicks*
25	*scripts off, and screams)* I knew it! You hate me! You think
26	we're all crazy! Right! You think we are all raving
27	maniacs! Lunatics! Is that it?
28	DIRECTOR: Hey, it's Hollywood. Some of my best friends
29	are lunatics.
30	CAT BURGLAR: *(Laughing like a maniac)* Yeah! Yeah! *(Begins*
31	*to lower gun)* Very good! You're all right — *(Quickly raises*
32	*his gun and points it at DIRECTOR)* for a two-bit Hollywood
33	director.
34	DIRECTOR: Thank you.
35	CAT BURGLAR: You're welcome. *(Jumps off desk and looks all*

1   *over floor for something, first tossing one script aside then another*
2   *one.)* **Where is it? Where!**
3   **DIRECTOR:**   **Can I help you?**
4   **CAT BURGLAR:**   *(Aiming gun at DIRECTOR, and screaming)* **No!**
5   **DIRECTOR:**   **Hey, OK. No problem.**
6   **CAT BURGLAR:**   *(Finally finds the script he's been looking for)*
7   **Found it!**
8   **DIRECTOR:**   **You found it? You mean you were looking for**
9   **a script?**
10   **CAT BURGLAR:**   **Not just a script. This script!**
11   **DIRECTOR:**   **What script is that?**
12   **CAT BURGLAR:**   **"The Psycho Cat Burglar Two!" I thought**
13   **you didn't make films about nutty cat burglars! You**
14   **promised me! You swore!** *(Screams as he jumps up and down*
15   *in a tantrum.)* **Liar! Liar! Your pants are on fire!**
16   **DIRECTOR:**   **Look! Look! I don't know how that script got in**
17   **there! Really!**
18   **CAT BURGLAR:**   **You're just saying that so I won't . . . you**
19   **know!**
20   **DIRECTOR:**   **No! No! I swear!**
21   **CAT BURGLAR:**   *(Paging through script to end)* **See! It's right**
22   **here in black and white! The crazy cat burglar aims gun**
23   **at** *(Aims gun at DIRECTOR's head)* **rogue cop's head and —**
24   **DIRECTOR:**   *(Screams)* **Don't shoot!**
25   **CAT BURGLAR:**   *(Pulls off ski mask and laughs)* **So . . . do I get**
26   **the part or not?**
27   **DIRECTOR:**   *(Looks at CAT BURGLAR)* **What?**
28   **CAT BURGLAR:**   **I said, do I get the part or not? What do you**
29   **think? How'd I do?**
30   **DIRECTOR: Wait a minute! Release me from these**
31   **handcuffs.** *(CAT BURGLAR does.)* **You crazy looney-bird.**
32   **Are you the actor who was coming in today to audition**
33   **for the part of the cat burglar?!**
34   **CAT BURGLAR: Yep. That's me.** *(Puts hand out to shake,*
35   *DIRECTOR shakes it weakly.)* **So was I convincing enough?**

1   Crrrraaaazy enough? Hmmmm? do I get the part?
2   DIRECTOR: Well ... actually I was thinking of someone else
3   for the part —
4   CAT BURGLAR: *(Pointing gun at DIRECTOR)* **What?**
5   DIRECTOR: *Don't shoot!(Ducking)* I was just mulling it over.
6   CAT BURGLAR: I hate that!
7   DIRECTOR: Wait! Don't shoot! We still have a part for you!
8   And please stop waving that gun in my face!
9   CAT BURGLAR: *(Laughs)* Hey. Relax. It's only a water pistol.
10   *(Shoots water into mouth)* **See?**
11   DIRECTOR: A water pistol?
12   CAT BURGLAR: Of course. I hate guns. So what's this other
13   part you've got for me?
14   DIRECTOR: Well, there's this wonderful character role. Can
15   you play a sadistic dentist? I mean a really, really sadistic
16   dentist?
17   CAT BURGLAR: **Sure!** *(Pulls a white coat out of bag and a dentist*
18   *mirror, runs over to DIRECTOR, leans DIRECTOR back in*
19   *chair.)* **Say awwwwww!** *(Lights go out as we hear sound of*
20   *dentist drill and DIRECTOR screaming.)*
21
22
23
24
25
26
27
28
29
30
31
32
33
34
35

Sherlock Holmes: 10 Minutes to Doom

PRODUCTION NOTES

PLAYERS: 2 males.

PLAYING TIME: About 12 minutes.

COSTUMES: HOLMES in his famous cloak and deerstalker's cap. WATSON in a black suit.

PROPERTIES: 2 pocket watches, rope, violin in case, piece of paper, mock bomb with small alarm clock.

LIGHTING EFFECTS: None.

SOUND EFFECTS: Loud and soft ticking of clock. Woman's scream from Offstage Right. A click.

Sherlock Holmes: 10 Minutes to Doom

CHARACTERS: SHERLOCK HOLMES; DR. WATSON.

Scene 1

TIME: The Gay 90s.

SETTING: HOLMES' Baker Street office. Old painting above fireplace on backdrop. On the left of the stage is a roll-top desk with papers and a chair. On the right of the stage is a sofa and small table with HOLMES' famous violin, which is safely in its case.

AT RISE: WATSON and HOLMES sit back to back. They are tied in two wooden chairs Center Stage. We hear a loud ticking.

WATSON: *(As ticking grows softer)* **It would seem we've met our end this time, Holmes.**

HOLMES: Elementary, my dear Watson.

WATSON: Holmes, I was wishing you wouldn't agree with me.

HOLMES: Well, Watson, old fellow, one can never call Sherlock Holmes dishonest. I fear this time we will become ... what is it they call it?

WATSON: Part of history? A bit of nostalgia?

HOLMES: I was thinking more of a blot on the ceiling — if of course there is any ceiling left after the explosion.

WATSON: Indeed.

HOLMES: Indeed, is indeed right. *(Trying desperately to wiggle free)* **Wiggle, Watson! Wiggle!**

WATSON: *(Wiggling, then stopping)* **It's no use, Holmes.**

HOLMES: I fear you're correct, old boy. That mad Moriority can certainly tie a dandy reverse, double-overlapped inverted Chinese strangulation square knot.

WATSON: I'll say. And he managed to do it several times, Holmes. I fear we are doomed. In ten minutes there will

1		be nothing left of the great Sherlock Holmes and his
2		faithful old sidekick, the kind, generous, and brilliant
3		old Dr. Watson. Nothing but atoms.
4	HOLMES:	Never fear, Watson. We still have nine minutes
5		and fifteen seconds left to free ourselves and locate
6		that . . . what was it we were looking for?
7	WATSON:	A bomb, Holmes! Can't you hear it ticking?
8	HOLMES:	Ah, yes. Elementary, Watson. Judging by the
9		sound of that ticking, I'd say it was definitely a time bomb.
10	WATSON:	Holmes! It is! Moriority said it was set to go off in
11		ten minutes. Which would mean we now have less than
12		nine minutes to live!
13	HOLMES:	The situation would seem utterly hopeless,
14		Watson. Would it not?
15	WATSON:	Yes, yes, Holmes. But I'm counting on you. You've
16		gotten us out of worse predicaments than this one.
17	HOLMES:	I have? Name one.
18	WATSON:	Holmes! There's no time for that now. We have to
19		free ourselves and locate that bomb before it blows us
20		and half the neighborhood to kingdom come.
21	HOLMES:	Yes, indeed, old boy. Try to wiggle your fingers.
22		Can you, old fellow?
23	WATSON:	No, Holmes. Moriority has made these ropes so
24		tight, I have lost all feeling in my hands.
25	HOLMES:	Funny.
26	WATSON:	I see nothing funny about it, Holmes. Nothing at
27		all. I cannot see where you would.
28	HOLMES:	It's just that my hands are perfectly well.
29		However, I have lost all feeling in my left leg. And then
30		there is the usual gout in the right one. I am not at all
31		comfortable, Watson, what with these ropes, this bomb,
32		and my bloody gout.
33	WATSON:	Gout? I didn't know you had gout, Holmes.
34	HOLMES:	There are quite a few things that you don't know
35		about me, Watson.

1	WATSON:	Like what?

1   WATSON: Like what?

2   HOLMES: Oh, many things. But I fear it may be too late now
3   for me to reveal less than a quarter of them. I shall begin
4   with the A's. Acne.

5   WATSON: Acne? I don't believe it, Holmes!

6   HOLMES: Alas, yes. The great Holmes was once called ... pizza
7   face.

8   WATSON: Holmes, no!

9   HOLMES: Yes.

10   WATSON: Simply amazing! I've been writing about you for
11   years. My dime novels have made your adventures and
12   you world famous. I thought I knew everything there was
13   to ever know about the great Sherlock Holmes.

14   HOLMES: Alas, no, old scribbler. Did you know, for instance,
15   that I am terrified of being blown to smithereens by small,
16   medium, or large-size bombs?

17   WATSON: Good gracious, Holmes. No! I did not know that!
18   I'm amazed! And here I thought you were absolutely
19   fearless!

20   HOLMES: I fear I am quite terrified, Watson. I may scream
21   for help any second now.

22   WATSON: You and me both! Do you have a plan, Holmes?

23   HOLMES: A plan?

24   WATSON: Yes. To free us and find that bomb.

25   HOLMES: No. Do you?

26   WATSON: Me? I'm just an old faithful sidekick. I know
27   nothing about plans. My forte is scribbling, fiction,
28   mystery, occasionally medicine. I know absolutely
29   nothing about plans. Especially plans of last-minute
30   escapes!

31   HOLMES: I was hoping you did, old fellow. For I fear we
32   have less than six minutes to destruction. I do hate to
33   see my dear old friend blown to bits.

34   WATSON: Holmes. I never even thought you cared one wit
35   about me.

1	HOLMES:	I wasn't referring to you, Watson, I was referring
2		to my dear old violin.
3	WATSON:	Your bloody fiddle?!
4	HOLMES:	Elementary, my dear Watson.
5	WATSON:	Blimey! And all I've done for you, Holmes. *(Trying*
6		*desperately to wiggle free)*
7	HOLMES:	Watson? What are you doing?
8	WATSON:	Trying to break free, Holmes. I don't wish to be
9		blown to eternity with you any longer.
10	HOLMES:	*(Suddenly pulls free and jumps up)* There will be no
11		need for that, old friend!
12	WATSON:	*(Is now able to pull himself free and stand)* Holmes!
13		How did you do it — and don't you dare say, "Elementary,
14		my dear Watson!"
15	HOLMES:	Er . . . then . . . um . . . let me put it this way. Well,
16		Watson, you see, Moriority failed to remember that while
17		I was in America several years ago on holiday, I managed
18		to find myself in the midst of a quite large gathering of
19		fishermen off the coast of Long Island.
20	WATSON:	Holmes, what in the name of heaven does a
21		gathering of fishermen have to do with freeing yourself
22		from these ropes.
23	HOLMES:	You see, Watson, *(As HOLMES ties a trick knot in*
24		*rope)* I had had my fill of the sights of New York, having
25		taken in every museum, library, art gallery, tall building,
26		including that wonderful lady in the harbor.
27	WATSON:	Holmes! I didn't know you dallied with ladies of
28		the . . . harbor.
29	HOLMES:	I'm talking about the Statue of Liberty, old fellow.
30	WATSON:	Ah, yes. Quite. A decent old gal.
31	HOLMES:	Indeed. And quite . . . how shall one put it . . .
32		large.
33	WATSON:	Indeed.
34	HOLMES:	Indeed. So, as I was saying, having surfeited my
35		appetite for mundane and novel tourist attractions, I

1   found myself discussing obscure knots.
2   WATSON: Obscure knots?
3   HOLMES: Exactly. Quite obscure knots. And the ordinary
4   variety such as your square, flat, double, slip, loop, cinch,
5   and — *(Puts the trick knot in front of WATSON's nose and*
6   *makes it disappear)* **trick!**
7   WATSON: Good lord! Amazing, Holmes! Simply amazing!
8   How did you do it, Holmes?
9   HOLMES: *(Tossing the rope away)* Elementary, my dear
10   Watson.
11   WATSON: I was afraid you'd say that.
12   HOLMES: Don't I always?
13   WATSON: You do, indeed, Holmes. You do indeed.
14   HOLMES: But, alas, old boy, I fear if we continue this
15   diatribe on obscure knots and past vacations, we will
16   shortly end in a very large puff of smoke.
17   WATSON: Good gracious! Yes, yes. I forgot! The bomb!
18   *(Checks his watch)* We must flee, Holmes, flee for our lives!
19   We have less than four minutes to doom! Quick! Let's get
20   out of here, Holmes!
21   HOLMES: Easier said than done, Watson.
22   WATSON: Why is that, Holmes? *(As HOLMES walks Offstage*
23   *Left)* Holmes, where are you going?
24   HOLMES: *(Exits Stage Left then returns, then exits Stage Right*
25   *and returns after WATSON has endured a few uncomfortable*
26   *seconds.)* Just as I thought.
27   WATSON: Thought what, Holmes? Where were you?
28   HOLMES: Checking the premises, old fellow.
29   WATSON: I see. And what did you find, Holmes?
30   HOLMES: I found that we are indeed doomed. You see, the
31   evil professor Moriority has sealed all the doors and
32   windows, and he has tied poor old Mrs. Hudson to the
33   newel post.
34   WATSON: Good heavens. The poor woman must be terrified.
35   HOLMES: Actually she was quite calm, Watson — that is

1   until I told her about the bomb.

2   **WATSON:**   Good lord. She must be in a panic!

3   **HOLMES:**   No. She's actually quite peacefully resting.

4   **WATSON:**   She is?

5   **HOLMES:**   Yes. Passed right out when I told her we had less
6   than four minutes to being vaporized by a very large time
7   bomb, which to my sensitive ears, is still ticking quite
8   strongly.

9   **WATSON:**   Yes! Yes! Holmes, can you find it in time?

10   **HOLMES:**   *(Shrugging)* Your guess is as good as mine, Watson.
11   But we can give it a bloody good try.

12   **WATSON:**   Yes. Excellent idea, Holmes. Have you got an idea
13   where that evil genius Moriority might have hidden the
14   dastardly thing?

15   **HOLMES:**   None at all, Watson.

16   **WATSON:**   Holmes! Think! You're famous for your brilliant
17   deductions!

18   **HOLMES:**   *(Pointing a finger at WATSON)* Ah, you see there,
19   old bean, that's where you're wrong.

20   **WATSON:**   *Wrong? What do you mean I'm wrong?*

21   **HOLMES:**   Old fellow, I barely know how to brew a cup of
22   tea let alone solve a clever crime.

23   **WATSON:**   *What?*

24   **HOLMES:**   Indeed. You see, Watson, without you to create in
25   your dandy little attempts at literary immortality these
26   truly ingenious solutions to the most baffling whodunits,
27   I would still be looking for my famous deer-stalker's cap.
28   *(Looking around)* Which I can never seem to locate when
29   I need the bloody thing.

30   **WATSON:**   Holmes, it's on your head.

31   **HOLMES:**   *(Touching, but not removing, the cap from his head and*
32   *looking at WATSON)* Elementary! Wonderful, Watson!
33   You're better at this detection game than even I!

34   **WATSON:**   *(Sitting on sofa, right on top of HOLMES' violin case)*
35   Blimey. I'm beginning to see that.

1	**HOLMES:**	*(Grabbing the violin case out from under WATSON,*
2		*who nearly ends up on floor)* **Oh, it's really quite true.**
3		**Without you to actually solve my crimes for me, and**
4		**without dear, old, terrified Mrs. Hudson to brew my tea**
5		**for me, I'd be nothing more than a fiddle-playing dandy.**
6		*(Is about to open the fiddle case)*
7	**WATSON:**	*(Jumps up in a panic)* **Holmes! Wait! Don't open that**
8		**case!**
9	**HOLMES:**	**Watson, why ever not? Are you trying to tell me**
10		**you detest my fiddle playing?** *(Opens the case as WATSON —*
11		*holding his ears — dives onto sofa.)*
12	**WATSON:**	***Holmes! The bomb could be in it!***
13	**HOLMES:**	*(Pulling out a fiddle)* **Nope. Just my dear old fiddle.**
14	**WATSON:**	*(Looking, lets his fingers drop from his ears until*
15		*HOLMES tries to play fiddle)* **Really?**
16	**HOLMES:**	*(Playing fiddle)* **Really. Watson, would you believe**
17		**I've never taken a single lesson?**
18	**WATSON:**	**Yes, Holmes.** *(Standing)* **But this is no time for**
19		**fiddling about. We do have a bomb to locate. Remember,**
20		**Holmes?**
21	**HOLMES:**	**Good heavens, old fellow, you're so right.** *(Putting*
22		*fiddle away)* **Forgive my temporary musical dalliance.**
23	**WATSON:**	**You're ... forgiven, Holmes. Now help me find**
24		**that bloody bomb.**
25	**HOLMES:**	**Yes, yes, old boy. How are we on time?**
26	**WATSON:**	*(Checking his watch)* **We have less than two minutes,**
27		**Holmes.**
28	**HOLMES:**	**I would say it looks rather bleak, Watson.**
29	**WATSON:**	*(As they look around quickly, bumping into each other)*
30		**Elementary, my dear Holmes. Good lord! Now he's got**
31		**me saying it!**
32	**HOLMES:**	*(Stopping)* **Watson! Wait! I have an idea!**
33	**WATSON:**	**Amazing, Holmes! Lately they are few and far**
34		**between. But as they say, I'm all ears!**
35	**HOLMES:**	*(Tapping WATSON's tummy)* **More like all tummy,**

1   old balloon.
2   WATSON: Just get to the point, Holmes.
3   HOLMES: Yes, yes. *(Pacing)* I think I'm onto something here,
4   old fellow.
5   WATSON: Yes, yes ... What, Holmes, what?
6   HOLMES: You say a bomb has been planted. Correct?
7   WATSON: No, no!
8   HOLMES: *(Stopping)* But I distinctly recall you saying that
9   there was a bomb that had been planted.
10   WATSON: Holmes! There is a bomb planted! But I didn't say it!
11   HOLMES: You didn't? Then who did?
12   WATSON: Moriority!
13   HOLMES: Ah! Yes! Elementary! Moriority. He is evil, ergo,
14   he would do something as dastardly as that.
15   WATSON: He is and he has. And if we don't find that bomb
16   in less than a minute, we'll be elementary! Elementary
17   particles!
18   HOLMES: Very clever, Watson! A pun, I believe. You always
19   did have a way with words.
20   WATSON: Thank you, Holmes.
21   HOLMES: Yes. A bloody terrible doctor, but a really quite
22   good dickerer with the King's English.
23   WATSON: I'd have to be to make an idiot like you the clever
24   dick that everyone thinks you are.
25   HOLMES: *(We hear a loud scream from Stage Right.)* Good lord!
26   What was that hideous sound?
27   WATSON: Mrs. Hudson has awoke.
28   HOLMES: Ah! For a second there I thought it was a horse
29   being rammed by one of those newfangled horseless
30   carriages.
31   WATSON: *(Checking his watch)* Yes! Yes, Holmes! But back to
32   the bomb! We have less than thirty seconds left!
33   HOLMES: We're doomed! *(Screams and falls over in a faint)*
34   WATSON: HOLMES!
35   HOLMES: *(Jumping up)* Just a bit of melodramatics there,

1   Watson, old fellow, designed to lighten the mood a twit.

2 WATSON: Speaking of twits, Holmes, you have fifteen
3   seconds to find that bomb, or I quit!

4 HOLMES: *(Running around in a panic, looking under sofa, behind*
5   *sofa, under painting, under chairs. Then suddenly HOLMES*
6   *gets an idea and runs to look inside desk, then quickly under*
7   *desk.)* **Good heavens! I do believe I'm stumped!**

8 WATSON: *(Handing HOLMES a piece of paper)* **Here, Holmes.**
9   **This is for you.**

10 HOLMES: *(Looking at it)* **What's this, Watson? A letter from**
11   **Mama?**

12 WATSON: Holmes, your mother disowned you fifteen years
13   ago when you failed to locate papa.

14 HOLMES: Then this must be —

15 WATSON: It's my bloody resignation, Holmes! Since you
16   failed to find the bomb, I quit! I refuse to be blown to my
17   final reward while in the employ of a half-wit!

18 HOLMES: WAIT! There is one place I haven't looked!

19 WATSON: *(Checking his watch)* **Hurry, Holmes!** *(As the ticking*
20   *grows louder)* **Ten, nine, eight . . .** *(As WATSON counts down,*
21   *HOLMES removes his cap and pulls out a small bomb.)* **Holmes!**
22   **It's the bomb! It's tiny — but deadly! Careful! Seven, six,**
23   **five —**

24 HOLMES: Elementary, my dear Watson! And I do believe
25   that this tiny, cleverly concealed red button here will . . .
26   *(WATSON ducks and holds his ears)* **turn it off.** *(We hear a*
27   *click and the ticking stops.)*

28 WATSON: Good show, Holmes! You've done it!

29 HOLMES: Rather simple, actually, old balloon.

30 WATSON: Elementary?

31 HOLMES: *(Looks at alarm clock of bomb)* **No, Watson, Swiss, I**
32   **believe.** *(Curtain falls as they both laugh.)*

33

34

35

A Death in the Family

PRODUCTION NOTES

PLAYERS: 2 males.

PLAYING TIME: About 10 minutes.

COSTUMES: MEDIC wears white hospital coat over his combat fatigues. SOLDIER is in full battle dress.

PROPERTIES: Chart, helmet, knapsack, canteen, rifle, bandages.

LIGHTING EFFECTS: None.

SOUND EFFECTS: Sound of hospital paging system and voice saying visiting hours are over. Sound of helicopter and its radio squarking out the words, "Man down! Man down!" Sound of gunfire.

SPECIAL EFFECTS: A great wind generated by landing helicopter.

A Death in the Family

CHARACTERS: MEDIC, a doctor; JONES, a soldier.

Scene 1

TIME: Now and then.

SETTING: A black stage. The backdrop can have a hospital emergency room scene projected onto it first then a battlefield scene projected onto it. Or the hospital scene can be painted on a curtain that can be raised to reveal the battlefield.

AT RISE: MEDIC stands Stage Front looking at a chart. We hear a hospital intercom paging doctors. We hear an announcement that visiting hours are over.

MEDIC: *(To audience)* **Hospitals are always hectic places. I work in the emergency room of a big city hospital. I patch up cuts and bruises, set broken arms and legs and generally repair bodies torn by knives and bullets. I also have the joyful or painful task of telling families whether or not their loved ones are going to live or die. It is no picnic. At times it can be emotionally exhausting. And I and the other doctors like me do this sometimes for thirty-six hours without a break. Oh, we catch a catnap now and then between heart attacks and bloody noses. We manage. Hey, it's a lot easier than Nam, Vietnam. There we had no time for even a catnap. I was a male nurse then.** *(As he talks, the SOLDIER enters in full combat gear. The backdrop fades from a hospital scene to a jungle clearing in Vietnam. The SOLDIER carries a rifle and is carefully walking across the stage, watching out for mines and snipers.)* **I got my gut training, shall we say, in Vietnam. I was fresh out of nursing school then. I was just a kid.** *(Suddenly the paging becomes the sound of helicopters and gunfire.)* **I grew up fast. We all did. We were like one big**

1   **family, each member watching out for the other. Black or**
2   **white, man or woman. We were all brothers and sisters back**
3   **then. I remember it as if it were yesterday. I especially**
4   **remember my first dying soldier.** *(SOLDIER stops. There is a*
5   *loud gunshot and SOLDIER screams and falls.)* **He was shot by**
6   **a sniper — probably a young kid himself, or a woman. The**
7   **soldier never saw him or her and probably was hit before**
8   **he even heard the shot coming from the enemy's hiding place**
9   **in the long grass or up in a tree.** *(The radio of the helicopter*
10   *squarks, "Man down! Man down!")* **I heard those words, "Man**
11   **down! Man down!" over my radio. Before I knew it,** *(MEDIC*
12   *drops the chart, removes his white hospital coat. Under it he is dressed*
13   *in combat fatigues. A helmet is thrown to MEDIC)* **they threw me**
14   **a helmet and I was in the war.**
15 **SOLDIER:**   **Medic! Medic! I'm hit! Help me!**
16 **MEDIC:**   *(Puts on a knapsack MEDIC is thrown, and MEDIC turns*
17   *and makes his way carefully back to Center Stage to SOLDIER.)*
18   **I was actually on my way to a field hospital Charlie**
19   **Company had set up to do what we could for the locals.**
20   **But then this G.I., halfway between headquarters and**
21   **the camp, was hit.**
22 **SOLDIER:**   **Help me! For God sake, help me!**
23 **MEDIC:**   **I could hear his screams across the rice paddies.**
24 **SOLDIER:**   **Somebody! Help me! Help! Please.**
25 **MEDIC:**   **He sounded like a kid right out of high school.**
26 **SOLDIER:**   **Help me! I'm dying!**
27 **MEDIC:**   **Actually, he was. Dying and just out of high school.**
28 **SOLDIER:**   **Don't let me die!**
29 **MEDIC:**   **I didn't know it then, but he was dying. He had been**
30   **hit real bad. Fatally.** *(MEDIC carefully approaches SOLDIER*
31   *as we hear gunfire.)* **By the time I got to him, he was deathly**
32   **pale and losing blood rapidly.**
33 **SOLDIER:**   **Medic! Oh, God.**
34 **MEDIC:**   *(MEDIC gets on his knees beside him and faces audience.)*
35   **I'm here, soldier.**

1   SOLDIER: Am I going to die? Is it bad?

2   MEDIC: *(To audience)* It wasn't bad. It was terrible. This was

3   not like the broken arms or legs I had studied. Or the

4   simple cuts and contusions. This I had never seen before.

5   *(MEDIC looks at SOLDIER's wounds, then to audience.)*

6   SOLDIER: Does it look bad?

7   MEDIC: *(To audience)* I had never seen anything like this

8   before. Never. Most people see TV crime shows. People

9   are shot left and right. You get to think you know what

10   a bullet can do to the human body. But you're wrong.

11   You have no idea what a piece of lead traveling at nearly

12   three times the speed of sound can do to flesh and bone.

13   SOLDIER: Help me! Oh, God.

14   MEDIC: *(To audience)* You have no idea of what the real thing

15   is like.

16   SOLDIER: I can't feel my arms or legs. Why can't I feel them?

17   Are they all right?

18   MEDIC: *(Trying to make SOLDIER comfortable by putting*

19   *MEDIC's knapsack under SOLDIER's head)* Yes, your arms

20   and legs are fine.

21   SOLDIER: Why can't I feel them? I don't feel them.

22   MEDIC: *(To audience)* What could I tell him? He would never

23   walk again? He would never be able to move his arms or

24   legs? He would never be able to feed himself or dress

25   himself?

26   SOLDIER: Why can't I move my arms or legs? Oh, God. No!

27   I can't move my arms or legs!

28   MEDIC: You've been shot. *(To audience)* As if he didn't know.

29   SOLDIER: I want to go home! Get me out of here!

30   MEDIC: The chopper is on its way.

31   SOLDIER: Where is it? I don't hear it!

32   MEDIC: It's coming.

33   SOLDIER: Why can't I move? I can't move.

34   MEDIC: *(To audience)* What could I tell him? He had been hit

35   just . . . in a bad spot. Actually the bullet had entered

1	seemingly in a non-vital area — through his upper arm,
2	passed through his left lung, and, maybe as he fell, moved
3	up, nicking his upper spine at just the right — or wrong —
4	angle. Not enough to kill him instantly, but just enough
5	to paralyze him from the neck down.
6	SOLDIER: I can't move! *(SOLDIER coughs and coughs.)*
7	MEDIC: He was beginning to have trouble breathing.
8	SOLDIER: Help me. *(SOLDIER coughs.)* I can't catch my
9	breath. I can't breathe.
10	MEDIC: Try to relax. What's your name, soldier?
11	SOLDIER: Jones. Randolph Jones. *(SOLDIER coughs.)* Am I
12	going to die? I don't want to die. Help me. Why can't I
13	breathe?
14	MEDIC: You've been hit in the lung. It's the blood. Just try
15	to breathe slowly. Your right lung is fine. *(To audience)* At
16	least I hoped it was.
17	SOLDIER: *(Coughs)* I'm choking. I can't breathe.
18	MEDIC: *(To audience)* There was nothing I could do. *(To*
19	*SOLDIER)* Relax. The chopper will be here in a few
20	minutes.
21	SOLDIER: I want to go home.
22	MEDIC: I know, Jones. That makes two of us. *(MEDIC gets*
23	*out a bandage and tries to stop the bleeding. To audience)* He
24	was losing a lot of blood. I had never seen so much blood.
25	I tried to stop the bleeding, but it just kept coming and
26	coming.
27	SOLDIER: I feel funny. I feel like I'm going to pass out.
28	MEDIC: Jones. Hang on. OK? Just a few more minutes. I'll
29	get you out of here. I promise. *(To audience)* I really wanted
30	to. He was getting weaker and weaker every minute. *(To*
31	*SOLDIER)* Relax. Breathe slowly. OK?
32	SOLDIER: Yeah. I'll try. What happened?
33	MEDIC: A sniper got you, probably from a tree or the grass.
34	You are wounded. So now you can go home. Pretty good,
35	huh? *(To audience)* I was praying he'd agree.

1   SOLDIER: Yeah. *(He coughs.)* I can't breathe.
2   MEDIC: Yes you can. Just relax.
3   SOLDIER: Am I going to die?
4   MEDIC: No. *(To audience)* I was always a good liar. But
5   medically speaking, I knew better. I figured in that heat
6   and humidity — it must have been a hundred and twenty
7   in the sun where we were — his heart would just not be
8   able to take the strain. I was doing all I could to breathe
9   in that jungle myself. And I had both my lungs and I
10   wasn't losing all my blood like this kid was.
11 SOLDIER: It's hot. Why is it so hot?
12 MEDIC: Here. *(MEDIC takes off his canteen and tries to give*
13   *SOLDIER a drink.)* Drink this. *(SOLDIER coughs.)* Easy.
14 SOLDIER: I want to go home.
15 MEDIC: Tell me about home, Jones. Where are you from?
16 SOLDIER: From New York. The Island.
17 MEDIC: Long Island?
18 SOLDIER: Yes. Since I was a kid.
19 MEDIC: Hey, we're   practically   neighbors.   I'm   from
20   Connecticut.
21 SOLDIER: I want to go home.
22 MEDIC: I know. Tell me about Long Island.
23 SOLDIER: It's my home.
24 MEDIC: I know. You went to school there?
25 SOLDIER: Yeah. Everything but college.
26 MEDIC: You went to college.
27 SOLDIER: No. I was going to go to college, but I got drafted.
28 MEDIC: What were you going to study in college?
29 SOLDIER: Study? I was a football player. I was going to play
30   football. I was a quarterback on the school team. I'm
31   gonna be a pro someday. Right?
32 MEDIC: Right. *(To audience)* He never made it. *(More gunfire,*
33   *MEDIC ducks, bending over SOLDIER.)* Another dream
34   shattered.
35 SOLDIER: Why can't I move my arms or legs? Why can't I move?

1	MEDIC: I don't want you to move. OK? Just relax. The Med-
2	Evac chopper is on its way.
3	SOLDIER: Tell it to hurry! Tell it to hurry.
4	MEDIC: *(To audience)* **They never did. Or at least that's the**
5	**way it always seemed. They were never there when you**
6	**needed them.**
7	SOLDIER: How long have I been here?
8	MEDIC: Not long. Just a few minutes.
9	SOLDIER: It seems like hours.
10	MEDIC: It just seems that way, Jones. *(To audience)* **It always**
11	**did. Minutes seemed like hours and hours seemed like**
12	**days. We lost a lot of kids just waiting for the choppers.**
13	SOLDIER: Where is that chopper? *(He coughs.)* Where is it?
14	MEDIC: It's on its way.
15	SOLDIER: I don't hear it.
16	MEDIC: It's coming. I promise. Just a few more minutes.
17	Hang in there.
18	SOLDIER: I'll try.
19	MEDIC: *(To audience)* **They all did. Look at the alternative.**
20	**No one wanted to be shipped home in a body bag.**
21	SOLDIER: I don't want to die.
22	MEDIC: You're not going to die. *(To audience)* **I lost count of**
23	**the number of times I used that line.** *(To SOLDIER)* **You're**
24	**not going to die.**
25	SOLDIER: You're just saying that.
26	MEDIC: No. Listen, Jones ... let's talk about Long Island.
27	OK?
28	SOLDIER: I want to go home.
29	MEDIC: What college were you hoping to go to after high
30	school?
31	SOLDIER: College?
32	MEDIC: Yes. You said you were planning to go to college
33	after you graduated high school, but you were drafted.
34	SOLDIER: College? Yeah. College. Right. I wanted to go to
35	Notre Dame or Fordham. I was drafted.

1   **MEDIC:**   So you'll go when you get back home. *(To audience)*

2   As I said, I was a good liar.

3   **SOLDIER:**   You're lying.

4   **MEDIC:**   *(To audience)* **Maybe not as good as I thought I was.**

5   *(To SOLDIER)* **What did you do in high school, besides**

6   **play football?** *(To audience)* **I was hoping he had something**

7   **he could do if he pulled through. He certainly wasn't**

8   **going to be playing football. Even if he made it back home.**

9   **Fat chance. But you could always hope. Some prayed.**

10   **SOLDIER:**   Oh, Jesus, please help me. Please.

11   **MEDIC:**   *(To audience)* **All I knew was that football was out.**

12   *(To SOLDIER)* **So tell me, besides football, what did you**

13   **like to do in high school?**

14   **SOLDIER:**   I loved track.

15   **MEDIC:**   *(To audience)* **Oh, great. Track.**

16   **SOLDIER:**   I used to run the hundred yard dash, the fifteen-

17   hundred and the marathon.

18   **MEDIC:**   No kidding. *(To audience)* **Actually, I was hoping he**

19   **liked something more sedentary, like a sit-down career**

20   **in accounting or computer programming. But if that**

21   **chopper didn't hurry, it wouldn't even come to that.**

22   **SOLDIER:**   Where is that chopper? I'm dying.

23   **MEDIC:**   No you're not. I won't let you die. *(To audience)* **My**

24   **other most used line. It still comes in handy.**

25   **SOLDIER:**   I feel like I'm going to pass out. I'm sorry.

26   **MEDIC:**   That's OK, kid. *(MEDIC holds his hand.)* **It's OK.**

27   **SOLDIER:**   I'm sorry.

28   **MEDIC:**   *(To audience)* **Some of them apologized as if this war,**

29   **their being wounded, was somehow their fault.**

30   **SOLDIER:**   Oh, God. I'm . . .

31   **MEDIC:**   *(To audience as MEDIC covers SOLDIER's face with*

32   *MEDIC's helmet)* **I can't really remember his name. I called**

33   **him Jones. But it could have been Smith, Ginzberg,**

34   **Peterson, or anyone of many.** *(MEDIC stands.)* **Anyway.**

35   **That's how I learned about life . . . and death. And where**

1   **I decided I wanted to be a doctor.** *(MEDIC sits Stage Front.)*
2   **I figured . . . we were all one big family and somebody**
3   **had to be there to hold a hand or tell an innocent little**
4   **white lie until the choppers came.** *(Sound of approaching*
5   *helicopter)* **Speaking of which . . .** *(MEDIC stands and waves*
6   *up over the audience to the chopper, yelling up to it.)* **Down**
7   **here!** *(Curtain falls as sound of chopper grows louder and wind*
8   *blows violently across stage.)*
9
10
11
12
13
14
15
16
17
18
19
20
21
22
23
24
25
26
27
28
29
30
31
32
33
34
35

PLAYS
FOR
WOMEN
ONLY

The Golden Door

PRODUCTION NOTES

PLAYERS: 2 females.

PLAYING TIME: About 15 minutes.

COSTUMES: MS. WILSON wears a business suit. ANNA has on a neat dress of some country.

PROPERTIES: File folders, pen, poem, clothes bags, reading glasses.

LIGHTING EFFECTS: None.

SOUND EFFECTS: None.

The Golden Door

CHARACTERS: ANNA, an immigrant woman; MS. WILSON, an interviewer at a U.S. Immigration Service Office.

Scene 1

TIME: Today.

SETTING: A sign hangs on the backdrop that reads U.S. IMMIGRATION SERVICE. There is a desk Stage Center behind which sits MS. WILSON. Her desk is piled high with file folders. There is a high pile of folders on her left and one on her right. Each is about two feet high. She barely has room to write. Between the piles of folders is a little name plaque that has on it MS. WILSON. A chair sits on the other side of the desk, at which ANNA will soon sit.

AT RISE: MS. WILSON is writing in a file folder. She looks annoyed by all this work. After a few long moments, she puts the file on top of the high pile of folders to her right. She then takes a folder from the high pile on her left.

MS. WILSON: *(She looks over the folder and shakes her head.)* **Another one. Everyone wants to be a U.S. citizen. They just keep coming and coming and coming.** *(Looks Offstage Left.)* **Next!** *(ANNA enters. MS. WILSON points to chair.)* **Have a seat . . .** *(Looking at name in folder)* **miss?** *(ANNA nods and sits quietly.)* **So you want to be an American, a U.S. citizen?**

ANNA: *(With an accent)* **Oh, yes. Yes, I do. Ever since I little girl, I want to be citizen of this wonderful country.**

MS. WILSON: **Yeah. That's what they all say.**

ANNA: **It not true?**

MS. WILSON: **True? What true — I mean, what's true?**

ANNA: **That this is a most wonderful country?**

MS. WILSON: *(Ironic)* **Oh, it's just great. Terrific.**

ANNA: **Yes. I know. Most terrific country in the world. One**

1   with the great golden door.
2   MS. WILSON: Golden door? What golden door?
3   ANNA: *(Surprised that MS. WILSON doesn't know which golden*
4   *door she means)* You know, the lady's door.
5   MS. WILSON: Lady? What lady?
6   ANNA: The big lady. Statue lady.
7   MS. WILSON: A lady that's a statue? *(Thinks, then)* Oh, yeah.
8   You mean the Statue of Liberty? Is that what you're
9   referring to?
10 ANNA: Yea. The big lady with the golden door.
11 MS. WILSON: I see. Well, I don't know about any golden door.
12   I sort of think if the door was gold, it would have been
13   ripped off by now, or, at the very least, covered with
14   graffiti.
15 ANNA: Ripped off? Oh, you mean by the big wind.
16 MS. WILSON: Not exactly. But, in fact, there is no golden
17   door that I know of. I think it's more like iron or wood.
18 ANNA: No, no. I have piece of paper that say it golden. *(ANNA*
19   *looks in her clothes bag and all her pockets for the paper. She*
20   *finds it in her breast pocket.)* I find it. I keep it safe right by
21   my heart.
22 MS. WILSON: *(Impatient, ironic)* Wonderful, terrific, but can
23   we get on with this interview? It's been a long day and
24   it's only . . . *(Checks her watch)* good lord, only nine-twenty-
25   five.
26 ANNA: You don't want to hear about the golden door?
27 MS. WILSON: It's really not one of the main priorities in my
28   life — unlike getting this interview over with. Do you
29   understand what I'm saying?
30 ANNA: *(Apologetic)* No. My English. It not too good.
31 MS. WILSON: So what else is new?
32 ANNA: *(Pointing to her, very excited)* Oh, I know! I know! New
33   York, New Jersey, New Mexico —
34 MS. WILSON: What?
35 ANNA: Yes. Yes. It very funny. A joke. I hear it on boat coming

1   to this great country. You like my joke?

2   MS. WILSON: *(Very bored)* I may die laughing.

3   ANNA: Yes. Yes. I, too. What new? New York, New Jersey —
4   very funny.

5   MS. WILSON: Yes, yes. Can we continue?

6   ANNA: Wait. Did you hear da one about the farmer's
7   daughter and the traveling salesman?

8   MS. WILSON: What?

9   ANNA: It's a joke. *(Bends over to whisper to MS. WILSON)* But
10   not as funny as "so what's new" joke. Actually my mother
11   didn't laugh at all. But you know mothers.

12   MS. WILSON: Yeah, you meet one mother, you meet them all.

13   ANNA: Yes. So about that golden door . . .

14   MS. WILSON: Are we still on that?

15   ANNA: Oh, yes. It very beautiful.

16   MS. WILSON: You know a door that is beautiful? Is that what
17   you're telling me?

18   ANNA: Yes. It true. No?

19   MS. WILSON: Next I'll probably hear the one about the
20   streets being paved with gold.

21   ANNA: *(Points to her)* Yes! I hear that, too.

22   MS. WILSON: I knew it.

23   ANNA: But it's not true.

24   MS. WILSON: It's not?

25   ANNA: No. You have to be very careful where you walk in
26   city street. Many dogs in this city. Many big dogs.

27   MS. WILSON: You found that out, did you?

28   ANNA: Yes. But to me streets are still paved with gold.

29   MS. WILSON: Really? How do you arrive at that conclusion?

30   ANNA: Many jobs. We all work. My brothers, my sisters, my
31   mother, my papa, my whole family. In our country no
32   jobs. Here — many jobs.

33   MS. WILSON: You do have your work permits?

34   ANNA: Work permit?

35   MS. WILSON: Yes. You, as an immigrant, are not allowed to

1   **work in this country without a permit. It's the law.**

2   **ANNA:**   But how do we eat or live if we can't work. None of

3   my family is lazy. We all work. It's the American way. No?

4   **MS. WILSON:**   Look, all I know is no permit, no work. Do you

5   understand?

6   **ANNA:**   No. Do you?

7   **MS. WILSON:**   *(Getting really annoyed)* It's not my job to

8   understand! My job is to enforce the immigration laws

9   of this country.

10   **ANNA:**   The land of the free and the home of the brave.

11   **MS. WILSON:**   Yeah, right. The one in which you need a

12   permit to work.

13   **ANNA:**   You have one?

14   **MS. WILSON:**   Do I have what?

15   **ANNA:**   This work permit.

16   **MS. WILSON:**   I don't need one. I'm a citizen. You're not.

17   **ANNA:**   Oh. So where I get this wonderful permit? Through

18   the golden door?

19   **MS. WILSON:**   Cute. Very cute. Listen, do you know we can

20   deport you for not having a work permit? Do you realize

21   that?

22   **ANNA:**   But everyone is entitled to life, liberty and the

23   pursuit of happiness in this great country. Right?

24   **MS. WILSON:**   That's what they tell me.

25   **ANNA:**   There. You see. And to my whole, entire family, work

26   is happiness. Is this not true?

27   **MS. WILSON:**   Look, I don't know anything about

28   happiness —

29   **ANNA:**   *(Cutting her off, shocked)* You don't? But you so lucky.

30   You are citizen. You have job. You have office that is your

31   office. You have much happiness. It is not true?

32   **MS. WILSON:**   *(Pages through the folder)* Can we please get on

33   with this interview? Is that all right with you?

34   **ANNA:**   You're the boss. No?

35   **MS. WILSON:**   I'm beginning to wonder.

1 ANNA: I have to tell you about the golden door.

2 MS. WILSON: I don't have the time. Do you see all these files?

3 *(ANNA nods.)* All right. Well, these are just today's. I have

4 a lot of people out there waiting to get in here. They all

5 want to be citizens. Do you understand?

6 ANNA: Oh, yes. They all want to be citizen of this great

7 country. From when we were little children we hear

8 stories about Miss Liberty and life, freedom, the great

9 golden door. Yes. I understand this very well. But do you?

10 MS. WILSON: What do you mean, do I? I'm an American, a

11 citizen. Of course, I understand. What makes you think

12 I don't?

13 ANNA: The way you speak about us. You sound like you don't

14 like us.

15 MS. WILSON: What ever gave you that idea?

16 ANNA: You don't speak to me very nice. My name is right

17 there. But you don't say, "Hello, Anna, welcome to our

18 wonderful country where the streets are paved with gold,

19 where there is a wonderful Statue of Liberty that

20 welcomes you, where there is life, liberty, and the pursuit

21 of happiness. Where there is a golden door. We welcome

22 you, Anna." You don't say that, Ms. Wilson. You sound so

23 unhappy. But you should be happy to live where these

24 things exist. They are not everywhere.

25 MS. WILSON: Look, Anna, it's just that I'm — what am I

26 trying to explain myself to you for? Just let me get to the

27 questions I have to ask you.

28 ANNA: But why don't you answer my question? You like it

29 here?

30 MS. WILSON: Yes. Where else can I shop in Bloomingdale's,

31 Macy's and Sears — and still not find the right blouse?

32 ANNA: Huh?

33 MS. WILSON: Never mind. It was just a joke.

34 ANNA: Well, not as funny as farmer's daughter joke. But not

35 bad ... maybe a six or seven, as jokes go.

1   MS. WILSON: Thanks.
2   ANNA: You welcome.
3   MS. WILSON: *(Beginning to soften)* **Look, Anna** . . . I don't mean
4   to be rude, but I have a job to do —
5   ANNA: Yes. You are the doorkeeper.
6   MS. WILSON: What?
7   ANNA: Yes. You are the doorkeeper, to the golden door.
8   MS. WILSON: Oh, I give up. Will you get it through your
9   head that there is no such thing as a golden door.
10 ANNA: *(Holding up paper)* But it says so right here. Miss Emma
11   Lazarus says so.
12 MS. WILSON: Who the devil is Emma Lazarus?
13 ANNA: You don't know Emma Lazarus? America's greatest
14   poet?
15 MS. WILSON: I thought Longfellow was.
16 ANNA: Who?
17 MS. WILSON: Never mind.
18 ANNA: OK. I tell you who Emma Lazarus is.
19 MS. WILSON: But —
20 ANNA: Wait, wait. You like her. She wrote this poem.
21 MS. WILSON: I must put a stop to this right now. We do not
22   have time for a poetry reading. This is the busiest
23   immigration office in the country —
24 ANNA: And you don't know who Emma Lazarus is?! *(Does*
25   *"shame, shame" gesture with her finger)* **Shame, shame, Ms.**
26   **Wilson.** You should have big copy of this poem on your
27   door.
28 MS. WILSON: My door?
29 ANNA: Yes. Your door. It is the golden door. No?
30 MS. WILSON: Well, I never looked at it that way.
31 ANNA: That's because you are on this side of it. You are
32   inside looking out. We, out there, are outside. We are
33   looking in.
34 MS. WILSON: Listen, why don't we just begin the interview.
35   OK?

1	ANNA: You the boss.
2	MS. WILSON: You sure?
3	ANNA: You have a big office. All these folders. You must be
4	a boss. No?
5	MS. WILSON: Me? I am the low man on the totem pole around
6	here.
7	ANNA: Low man? You not a woman?
8	MS. WILSON: No, no.
9	ANNA: You a man?!
10	MS. WILSON: No, I am a woman! "Low man on the totem
11	pole" is just an expression. Like "land of the free and the
12	home of the brave," or "life, liberty, and the pursuit of
13	happiness," even "the golden door." They are all just
14	expressions.
15	ANNA: No, no. They are the truth. You just don't see this.
16	MS. WILSON: *(Checking her watch)* All I see is that it's getting
17	late and we have to get on with this interview — golden
18	door or no golden door.
19	ANNA: Funny you should mention golden door. *(Unfolds her*
20	*poem)*
21	MS. WILSON: Oh, no. You're not going to give me a poetry
22	reading, are you?
23	ANNA: I do my best. But I no Emma Lazarus.
24	MS. WILSON: I'm not so sure of that.
25	ANNA: Oh, Ms. Wilson, what a nice thing to say. Thank
26	you.
27	MS. WILSON: You're welcome. So . . . you going to read that
28	so we can start this interview?
29	ANNA: If you insist.
30	MS. WILSON: Oh, please, please. I am all ears.
31	ANNA: *(Looking at her ears)* No. You have nice little ears.
32	MS. WILSON: It was just another expression.
33	ANNA: Oh. You have a lot of them. Don't you?
34	MS. WILSON: Hey, it's America. Right?
35	ANNA: You are right. America has much of everything.

1   MS. WILSON: Especially expressions.
2   ANNA: You ain't whistling Dixie.
3   MS. WILSON: *(Pointing at ANNA)* **Very good.**
4   ANNA: See. I make a good American. No?
5   MS. WILSON: I must admit, you do seem to like this country.
6   ANNA: No. I love her. And Emma Lazarus. She must have
7   been a wonderful lady. She work here like you maybe?
8   MS. WILSON: *(Melting)* **Well, not exactly, Anna.**
9   ANNA: Oh, well. Maybe she too busy with her poetry. I read
10   for you what she write. OK?
11   MS. WILSON: OK, Anna. You do that.
12   ANNA: I do that, Ms. Wilson. *(ANNA stands and puts on her*
13   *glasses then reads lovingly.)*
14   The New Colossus
15   Not like the brazen giant of Greek fame,
16   With conquering limb astride from land to land;
17   Here at our sea-washed, sunset gates shall stand
18   A mighty woman with a torch, whose flame
19   Is the imprisoned lightening, and her name
20   Mother of exiles, from her beacon-hand
21   Glows world-wide welcome; her mild eyes command
22   The air-bridged harbor that twin cities frame,
23   'Keep ancient lands, your storied pomp!' cries she
24   With silent lips, 'Give me your tired, your poor,
25   Your huddled masses yearning to breathe free,
26   The wretched refuse of your teeming shore,
27   Send these, the homeless, tempest-tost to me,
28   I lift my lamp beside the golden door!
29   So what do you think? OK?
30   MS. WILSON: Yes. OK.
31   ANNA: You like?
32   MS. WILSON: I like very much. In fact, I would like to make
33   a copy of that and hang it on my door.
34   ANNA: Right. The golden door. *(Offers MS. WILSON the poem)*
35   MS. WILSON: Yes. *(Takes poem)* **I guess we sort of take a lot**

1   of this for granted after being here a while.
2   ANNA: Not me.
3   MS. WILSON: I guess not.
4   ANNA: So, Ms. Wilson, I make a good citizen?
5   MS. WILSON: Yes. I'm sure.
6   ANNA: Oh, good. Ms. Wilson, can I ask you a question?
7   MS. WILSON: Well, actually, I am supposed to be asking you
8   the questions, Anna, but . . . what the heck, go ahead.
9   Shoot.
10   ANNA: Shoot?! But I have no gun — *(She sees MS. WILSON*
11   *smiling)* Oh —
12   ANNA and MS. WILSON: *(Together)* An expression!
13   MS. WILSON: Exactly. So what's your question, Anna?
14   ANNA: About the golden door.
15   MS. WILSON: What about it?
16   ANNA: Some people say they are going to put a lock on it.
17   Is this true? Is the golden door going to have a lock put
18   on it? *(They look at each other in silence as the curtain falls.)*
19
20
21
22
23
24
25
26
27
28
29
30
31
32
33
34
35

My Baby

PRODUCTION NOTES

PLAYERS: 2 females.

PLAYING TIME: About 10 minutes.

COSTUMES: KATE has on a nightgown and robe. MIRIAM has on jeans and blouse.

PROPERTIES: None.

LIGHTING EFFECTS: None.

SOUND EFFECTS: Sound of hospital intercom paging doctors. Bette Midler's song "You Gotta have Friends."

My Baby

CHARACTERS: KATE, a surrogate mother; MIRIAM, her best
friend.

Scene 1

TIME: Today.

SETTING: A lounge in a hospital. There is a sign that reads
MATERNITY WARD with an arrow pointing Stage Left. There
is a NO SMOKING sign and we can hear the intercom paging
doctors.

AT RISE: KATE and MIRIAM are sitting on a couch, not talking,
but looking straight ahead.

MIRIAM: Katie?

KATE: No. I just can't. I just cannot. I'm sorry, Miriam. I
know I promised you, but I just can't.

MIRIAM: But you said —

KATE: I know what I said. I know I promised you and Peter.
But when I saw her this morning, when I held her in my
arms.

MIRIAM: But we're friends. You promised. You're my best
friend. All these years we've been friends. Since we were
kids. And you've never broken a promise. Never. Not to
me.

KATE: Don't you think I know that?

MIRIAM: *(Gets up and paces)* We were always best friends. We
always helped each other out. We were always there for
each other. Remember?

KATE: Yes. I know.

MIRIAM: I don't think you do. I think you've forgotten.
That's what I think. Just like that, you've forgotten.

KATE: I haven't forgotten, Miriam. How could you say that?
How could I forget? God, we're like sisters.

1　MIRIAM: More than sisters. I told you things I never told
2　　　　my sisters. I know it sounds corny, but we were like soul
3　　　　mates, kindred spirits. God, you're lucky you're not a
4　　　　man, because I would have married you instead of Peter.
5　KATE: Heaven help us.
6　MIRIAM: Don't joke. It's not funny. We were so close.
7　KATE: We still are. I still love you. *(She stands and goes to put*
8　　　　*her arm on MIRIAM's shoulder, but MIRIAM pulls away.)*
9　　　　Miriam?
10　MIRIAM: You promised! How could you do this to me? How
11　　　　could you?
12　KATE: *(Sitting back down)* I don't know. I didn't think I would,
13　　　　especially not having a husband — or a boyfriend, for
14　　　　that matter. But then I saw her.
15　MIRIAM: I saw her, too. How do you think I feel? Do you
16　　　　have any idea how I feel, Kate? Do you?
17　KATE: I know. It must hurt.
18　MIRIAM: Hurt? That's an understatement. After all these
19　　　　months of planning and dreaming and waiting. Did you
20　　　　do any of that?
21　KATE: Well . . . No, I guess not . . . But . . .
22　MIRIAM: But what?
23　KATE: But . . . I don't know. I did want to give you something,
24　　　　I was doing it for you, but . . .
25　MIRIAM: But what? You're telling me you weren't sure even
26　　　　then?
27　KATE: I thought I was. When you asked me that night at my
28　　　　place, remember how I hugged you? *(MIRIAM nods.)* I
29　　　　thought, wow, what a great idea. And you picked me. I
30　　　　was so happy. I think I loved you more than . . . than ever
31　　　　before. I was so happy.
32　MIRIAM: Yeah. So was I.
33　KATE: Oh, Mir, I so much wanted to make you happy. I
34　　　　thought what a sweet thing to do for my best friend. This
35　　　　was like the ultimate gift, you know?

1 MIRIAM: I thought I knew.

2 KATE: *(She gets up and paces.)* **You did. We both did. What**
3 **more could I do for the friend who always stood by me**
4 **when guys dumped me or when my parents were killed.**
5 **It was always you. You were always there for me. Right?**

6 MIRIAM: You were my friend.

7 KATE: I still am! I still love you. It's just that I love her
8 too . . . I can't give her up.

9 MIRIAM: Katie, it wouldn't be like you'd never see her again.
10 Hey, we practically live together. We're together more
11 than Peter and I. So you'd always be there — now for
12 both of us, instead of just me.

13 KATE: Miriam, I can't.

14 MIRIAM: You can't what? You can't give her to me or we
15 can't be friends anymore?

16 KATE: Please don't say that. *(KATE sits down.)* **You know we'll**
17 **always be friends.** *(MIRIAM turns her back on KATE.)*
18 **Miriam? Right? We'll always be friends? Miriam? Say**
19 **something.**

20 MIRIAM: What is there left to say?

21 KATE: Say you still love me. Say we're still friends. Please.
22 I need you — especially now.

23 MIRIAM: Why would you need me if you have her?

24 KATE: I'll always need you. Hey, you know me. Who'd take
25 the knots out of my sneakers if I lost you? Huh? Half the
26 time I can't do anything right.

27 MIRIAM: Well, you sure made a beautiful baby.

28 KATE: *(She smiles.)* **I did, didn't I?**

29 MIRIAM: You sure did. And you promised her to me.

30 KATE: I know. *(Stands up and goes over to MIRIAM who walks*
31 *to the other side of stage)* **Miriam, don't do this to me. Don't**
32 **do this to us.**

33 MIRIAM: I'm not the one who's doing it.

34 KATE: And I am?

35 MIRIAM: You're the one who broke her promise.

1	KATE: Miriam, what about me? Don't you think I know I
2	hurt you? How do you think I feel?
3	MIRIAM: All I know is that you made a promise. You've never
4	broken a promise before. Never. I trusted you.
5	KATE: I know you did. And I never meant to hurt you. It's
6	just that after carrying her all these months, and then
7	seeing her this morning, holding her. Have you held her
8	yet?
9	MIRIAM: They wouldn't let me.
10	KATE: *(Walking over to MIRIAM)* Why not?
11	MIRIAM: They said only the mothers could hold the babies.
12	KATE: I'll talk to the nurse.
13	MIRIAM: No. That's all right.
14	KATE: You don't want me to talk to the nurse? Or you don't
15	want to hold her?
16	MIRIAM: I don't know . . . I don't know. When I see her I
17	practically . . . Now, after you did this, if I held her . . .
18	KATE: But she'll love you, just like I do. Hey, you'll be like
19	her second mom. Really. You'll see.
20	MIRIAM: *(Sitting on couch)* I'm really upset by all of this, Katie.
21	KATE: *(Sitting beside her)* I know. Mir, believe me, the last
22	thing in the world I ever wanted to do was hurt you, hurt
23	my best, my dearest friend.
24	MIRIAM: Well, you sure did. You have no idea. I used to
25	dream about this day, when I'd hold her for the first time.
26	And all the things her and Peter and I would do.
27	KATE: You and Peter and her?
28	MIRIAM: Oh, you'd be there, too. Like always. I promise.
29	KATE: *(Pulling away to other side of couch)* I feel terrible.
30	MIRIAM: You want to throw up?
31	KATE: The ache is not in my stomach. It's in my heart. It's
32	breaking. I don't want to lose you over this. It's not fair.
33	MIRIAM: Fair? When is anything fair? Life's not fair. It's not
34	fair your parents were killed in that plane crash, it's not
35	fair that half the world goes to bed hungry, it's not fair

1   that I can't have kids. Fair? What's fair?
2   KATE: I tried. I really did. Miriam?
3   MIRIAM: Katie, how could you do this to me after all I did
4   for you? After all Peter and I did?
5   KATE: *(KATE stands up and paces.)* If you're trying to make
6   me feel guilty, you have.
7   MIRIAM: *(Walks over to KATE)* Who paid all your doctor bills
8   for the last nine months?
9   KATE: You and Peter.
10   MIRIAM: You're darn right. And who held you when you
11   barfed up your guts every morning?
12   KATE: You did?
13   MIRIAM: Right. God! I never saw anyone barf so much in
14   my life, but did I run and hide when you were so sick?
15   KATE: No, you never did, Miriam.
16   MIRIAM: You're darn right I didn't. Because I loved you and
17   wanted to be there for you. And I always was. Right?
18   KATE: Yes, yes, yes. What can I say? I'm a no-good rat. I
19   deserve to be ... to be ... I don't know ... whatever they
20   do to no-good rats is probably too good for me. I feel
21   terrible, but what can I do about it?
22   MIRIAM: You can give me your baby.
23   KATE: *(Pointing at her)* See?
24   MIRIAM: See what?
25   KATE: What you said. You called it *my* baby.
26   MIRIAM: Well, so ...?
27   KATE: Even you instinctively feel that. And so do I. It's my
28   baby. It's like part of me, part of my very being. Part of
29   my heart. Can I give my heart away?
30   MIRIAM: You sure had no trouble giving it away to all those
31   guys.
32   KATE: That's not the same thing, and you know it.
33   MIRIAM: Look, all I know is that you signed all those papers
34   and we paid all your doctor bills, and I took care of you.
35   KATE: Miriam, I'll pay you back. I promise. Every penny.

1	MIRIAM:	Sure. Where will you get the money?
2	KATE:	I have a job.
3	MIRIAM:	A job? You call the popcorn girl at the local X-rated
4		movie theater a job?
5	KATE:	Sure. What would you call it?
6	MIRIAM:	A temporary inconvenience, like all the other jobs
7		you've had.
8	KATE:	At least I work.
9	MIRIAM:	Now what is that supposed to mean? Because I
10		stay home and take care of the house while Peter works
11		I'm no good? Is that what you're saying?
12	KATE:	No, no, no. Look, I promise I'll pay you back.
13	MIRIAM:	The money is not important. I don't care about the
14		money, all right? It's the baby. You promised you'd give
15		her to me. You promised.
16	KATE:	I know.
17	MIRIAM:	When you heard I couldn't have kids you promised
18		to give me a baby.
19	KATE:	I know. You were so depressed. I hate it when you're
20		like that. I felt so heartbroken for you. It was the only
21		thing I could think of to help you. Maybe I didn't know
22		what I was getting into.
23	MIRIAM:	Maybe.
24	KATE:	Right. You know me. I'm like a kid at times. I can't
25		stand it when anyone is hurt. I can't even step on a bug.
26		Remember that time you were terrified by that water
27		bug? We saw it crossing your kitchen floor. You jumped
28		up on a chair and screamed to me, "Kill it! Kill it!" And
29		all I could do was sweep it out the door into the garden?
30	MIRIAM:	I remember.
31	KATE:	So you know if I couldn't hurt a water bug I could
32		never hurt my dearest friend. *(MIRIAM is silent.)* **Miriam?**
33		**Do you believe me?** *(KATE lays her hand on MIRIAM's back.)*
34		**Miriam? You know I love you.**
35	MIRIAM:	*(Hugs KATE.)* I know. I'm sorry, Katie. I'm sorry!

1   KATE: *(As they hug each other)* **Me, too. I never wanted to hurt**
2   **you. You believe me? Don't you?**
3   MIRIAM: **I believe you. But I wanted that baby so much.**
4   KATE: *(Comforting her)* **I know, I know. I didn't think I'd ever**
5   **want a kid, but I do. I want this one. And I think now I**
6   **know why.**
7   MIRIAM: **Why?**
8   KATE: **Because I had it out of love for someone I love. I didn't**
9   **have it just for me, but for someone I really love. You**
10   **know what I mean?**
11   MIRIAM: **I guess.**
12   KATE: **I promise you, Mir, you're going to be like a second**
13   **mom to this kid. Hey, who's going to babysit while I go**
14   **back to college, huh?**
15   MIRIAM: **Me?**
16   KATE: **If you want.**
17   MIRIAM: **Of course I do.**
18   KATE: **Good, because now that I have someone who needs**
19   **me, my days as popcorn girl at the Pink Pussycat are over.**
20   MIRIA: **So what are we going to name her?**
21   KATE: **I was thinking of calling her Miriam.**
22   MIRIAM: **After me?**
23   KATE: **Who else?**
24   MIRIAM: **Can I hold her?**
25   KATE: **You want to?**
26   MIRIAM: **I do now.**
27   KATE: **Good. I love ya, Mir.**
28   MIRIAM: **I love you too, Katie.** *(They walk Offstage Left to*
29   *maternity ward holding hands as Bette Midler's song "You Gotta*
30   *Have Friends" plays and curtain falls.)*
31
32
33
34
35

The Day Mother Left Home

PRODUCTION NOTES

PLAYERS: 2 females.

PLAYING TIME: About 10 minutes.

COSTUMES: MOTHER wears a housecoat and slippers. PAULA wears a business suit.

PROPERTIES: TV remote-control unit, wheelchair, 2 white sheets, keys.

LIGHTING EFFECTS: The lights dim out at the end of the play and a spotlight focuses on PAULA.

SOUND EFFECTS: Sound of a door closing.

The Day Mother Left Home

CHARACTERS: MOTHER, a very independent woman; PAULA, MOTHER's daughter.

Scene 1

TIME: Today.

SETTING: The parlor of MOTHER's house. Old furniture, a Persian rug, candelabra, doilies, old photographs. Old clock on backdrop. Old sofa sits Stage Center. TV set sits Downstage Right. Everything should suggest a house that has seen better days.

AT RISE: MOTHER sits Downstage Left in wheelchair facing audience. PAULA sits on sofa. They are not happy. Neither looks at the other or knows what more to say. They have been like this for a while.

MOTHER: *(After a few moments)* **I simply refuse to go. You can't make me.**

PAULA: **Mother. Please don't do this. I just can't handle it any longer. I've tried. But it's getting to me. Can't you see that? Can't you see I just can't handle it any longer?**

MOTHER: **What can't you handle? Tell me. What can't you handle?**

PAULA: **The fact that I go to work every day and you're here at home all alone.**

MOTHER: **So? So why is that a big problem?**

PAULA: **What if there's a fire? What if a burglar breaks in?**

MOTHER: **I'll say, "Hi, Mr. Burglar, can I help you?" Maybe I'll make him some tea or coffee. We'll talk. Have a bagel.**

PAULA: **Very funny. And what if he wants more than tea or coffee or a bagel?**

MOTHER: **I'll make him a blintz.**

PAULA: **Mother, this is not funny. What if —**

1 MOTHER: What if... what if...! What if we have an
2   earthquake or the house is struck by lightning? Huh?
3   You ever think of that? *(She wheels over to straighten a doily*
4   *on the sofa.)*
5 PAULA: It's a possibility.
6 MOTHER: And so is a tidal wave. But do you know how long
7   it's been since we've had a tidal wave in Kansas?
8   *(Straightening other doilies)* All the doilies are always
9   crooked.
10 PAULA: Mother. I'll do that. *(Gets up and tries to help. MOTHER*
11   *gently slaps her hand away.)* Mother, don't do that. I'll do it.
12 MOTHER: I can still keep my house clean.
13 PAULA: You had a stroke. You're supposed to take it easy.
14 MOTHER: You take it easy. I like to keep moving. You stop
15   moving, then you're in trouble.
16 PAULA: If you don't rest, you'll end up —
17 MOTHER: In that nursing home? Is that what you were going
18   to say? Well, I will not go there. This is my home. I live
19   here. You can go to the nursing home if you want, but I
20   am staying here.
21 PAULA: *(Paces)* And what if you fall out of your chair while
22   I'm out at work?
23 MOTHER: *(Pulls out a TV remote-control unit from her pocket)*
24   That's why I carry the TV's remote-control unit with me
25   at all times. I fall, all I do is hit the button and watch the
26   soaps till you get home.
27 PAULA: And what if you should hurt yourself when you fall?
28 MOTHER: *(Putting the remote-control unit back in her pocket)*
29   There you go again. What if, what if. Paula, you worry
30   too much. That's not good for you. You want to end up
31   with a stroke?
32 PAULA: If I worry, it's because I love you and I don't want
33   you to get hurt.
34 MOTHER: Sit. *(PAULA sits on sofa. MOTHER holds her hands.)*
35   I won't get hurt. I promise. OK? I'll be very careful. No

1	more sky diving or mountain climbing. OK? You happy?
2	*(PAULA stands up and paces.)*
3	PAULA: Mother, be serious.
4	MOTHER: Serious-smirious. You're serious enough for both
5	of us. I want to be young and foolish. You take care of
6	the serious department. OK?
7	PAULA: Well, one of us has to. You certainly are not.
8	MOTHER: The last time I was serious, I had a stroke. From
9	now on I'm going to be the life of the party. But don't
10	worry. I'll be careful. I promise I won't dance naked on
11	the piano with the lampshade on my head anymore. OK?
12	I'll be careful. *(Crosses her fingers behind her back so PAULA*
13	*can't see it, but audience should.)*
14	PAULA: You said that last time and I came home to find you
15	on the floor.
16	MOTHER: I was watching TV. I was there for five minutes.
17	PAULA: That's what you say.
18	MOTHER: What? You don't believe your mother?
19	PAULA: How can I? The doctor tells you to rest, and I find
20	you in the street in your chair dodging cars.
21	MOTHER: I was not dodging cars. They were dodging me.
22	PAULA: You could have been killed.
23	MOTHER: I'd rather be killed by some maniac driver out to
24	run down a poor, sweet little old lady in a wheelchair,
25	than by the total boredom in some antiseptic nursing
26	home ward.
27	PAULA: They don't have wards at the home. Everyone has
28	their own room.
29	MOTHER: I have my own room here. I like it. I like the way
30	it smells. Like old roses. You ever smell the inside of a
31	nursing home?
32	PAULA: Yes. And it smells very clean.
33	MOTHER: It smells very clean like a dentist office smells
34	very clean. And I have no intention of spending my golden
35	years in no dentist office.

1   PAULA: You're exaggerating.

2   MOTHER: Will you stop pacing and sit down?

3   PAULA: *(PAULA sits on sofa.)* All I'm saying is that you'll get
4   to like it.

5   MOTHER: What? Like I got to like the way you make liver
6   and onions? Or the way I got to like taking cod-liver oil
7   every morning? *(Holds her nose and shivers)* Yuck.

8   PAULA: No. I mean you'll have people to talk to and be with.
9   They play cards at the home — and mahjongg.

10   MOTHER: Woop-dee-do!

11   PAULA: You won't be alone.

12   MOTHER: Alone? Who's alone? I have you. Then there's Mr.
13   Johnson, the mailman, Bobbie, the paperboy.
14   Occasionally I get an obscene phone call or a wrong
15   number. My day is full. I'm never bored. Cards bore me.
16   Mahjongg is a pain in the butt. So I'll stay here, thank you.

17   PAULA: I just don't know.

18   MOTHER: You don't know what?

19   PAULA: What if I got in an accident on the way home from
20   work? Or what if I have to spend a week out of town?
21   You know I might with my new position down at the
22   office. How will you shop?

23   MOTHER: So we'll stock up on TV dinners and buy a
24   microwave. I'll order pizza. They deliver, you know.

25   PAULA: No way. Mother, there is no way I could be any good
26   half way across the country at some conference if I knew
27   you were home alone with nothing to eat but some
28   microwave TV dinner or some cold pizza.

29   MOTHER: They are never cold. They deliver them in a
30   special box. If you get a cold pizza, they don't charge — or
31   you get a free gallon of coke. Something like that.

32   PAULA: Terrific.

33   MOTHER: Paula, don't you see?

34   PAULA: See what?

35   MOTHER: That all these fears you have about me are

1   your fears. They are your problem; not mine. Don't you

2   see? You worry too much.

3 PAULA: You're darn right I worry! You're my mother and I

4   worry about you because I love you.

5 MOTHER: I know. I know. But I can take care of myself. Just

6   give me a chance. None of you do. Not the doctors. Not

7   the nurses. Look, just because I'm in a wheelchair

8   suddenly I'm no good? I'm helpless? What about all those

9   women in wheelchairs who have kids and take care of

10   their house? And that girl in the wheelchair that was in

11   "Playboy".

12 PAULA: Oh, so now you're going to be in "Playboy"?

13 MOTHER: Hey, the way they make you up, I'd probably look

14   pretty good. I'm not that old, you know. I'll drop Hef a

15   line while you're away. I'll let you know what he says.

16 PAULA: Look, Mom, they are young. You're not.

17 MOTHER: Thanks a lot. You're only as old as you feel.

18 PAULA: You know what I mean.

19 MOTHER: You mean I'm a helpless old lady who should

20   resign herself to a life of pinochle and mahjongg. Well I

21   will not. Just because I had a stroke is no reason to put

22   me away. I'm still able to take care of myself.

23 PAULA: *(Gets up and walks around as she talks)* Who shops?

24   Who cleans house? Who cuts the grass? Who puts out the

25   garbage?

26 MOTHER: So who does?

27 PAULA: I do. That's who.

28 MOTHER: Who asked you? God, I try to straighten a doily,

29   and you pounce on me. *(Imitating her)* Oh, I'll get it, Mom!

30   Oh, Mother, don't strain yourself! Oh, I'll do this. Oh, I'll

31   do that. *(In her own voice)* You know, just because I can't

32   run the four-minute mile any longer doesn't mean I can't

33   keep a neat house. Besides, how are you going to afford

34   to put me in a nursing home? They are very expensive.

35 PAULA: *(Not wanting to tell her, then)* Don't worry. We can

1 afford it.
2 MOTHER: What did you do? Win the lottery?
3 PAULA: No.
4 MOTHER: Well, you certainly can't afford it on your salary,
5 not yet. The only way you can afford it is by selling the
6 house. *(Realizing this is just what PAULA is planning)* **Oh,**
7 **no! You're not going to sell my house. This is my house!**
8 PAULA: Mother, don't get excited.
9 MOTHER: *Excited?!* Who's excited? I'm furious! This is my
10 house! You can't sell it.
11 PAULA: I can't keep it up myself. And you can't help. I have
12 no more time. I have to work longer hours now that I've
13 been promoted. Besides, I have to move closer to the
14 office.
15 MOTHER: Have to or want to?
16 PAULA: *(Thinking)* A little of both, I guess.
17 MOTHER: Paula, I can't believe you're doing this to me.
18 PAULA: *(Sits on sofa, near MOTHER)* Mother, you make it
19 sound like I'm putting you in prison.
20 MOTHER: And what is that nursing home? A country club?
21 You see any tennis courts out there? You have no right
22 to put me in there.
23 PAULA: *(Stands, with her back to MOTHER)* I'm only doing
24 what I think is best.
25 MOTHER: Best for who? Me . . . or you?
26 PAULA: Best for both of us. You'll be safe and I'll be able to
27 sleep nights. It hasn't been easy for me.
28 MOTHER: It hasn't been a picnic for me, miss. You think
29 being in this chair is a picnic? This is no picnic, Paula.
30 *(She does a wheelie.)* Except when I do a wheelie.
31 PAULA: *(In a panic)* Mother! Be careful!
32 MOTHER: *(Spinning around)* Oh, relax. By the way, do they
33 have wheelchair basketball at that nursing home? Or just
34 basket weaving?
35 PAULA: They have a lot of things.

1   MOTHER: But probably not wheelchair basketball.

2   PAULA: They have trips to plays and museums. And even

3   the zoo.

4   MOTHER: Sounds like a wild time.

5   PAULA: You love the zoo.

6   MOTHER: Sure. Going with you I love it. But going with a

7   bunch of old fogies, no way José.

8   PAULA: Mother, you're really making this very difficult for

9   me. I really can't take much more of this. *(She sits on sofa*

10   *and puts her face in her hands.)*

11   MOTHER: Paula, you're like me. You're strong. You can take

12   it.

13   PAULA: *(Looking at her)* You're wrong. I'm not like you. I was

14   never like you.

15   MOTHER: Yes you are. You're very strong. And you're all I

16   have left. When I had this stroke your father left me. So

17   you're all I have.

18   PAULA: *(She stands.)* Mother, I cannot take this anymore.

19   Tomorrow we are going to look at that nursing home.

20   MOTHER: No I'm not.

21   PAULA: Yes you are.

22   MOTHER: No, I'm not!

23   PAULA: Yes you are!

24   MOTHER: *(Takes out the remote-control unit from her pocket)* You

25   want to watch TV, Paula. Maybe Phil Donahue will have

26   on those old folks who are into mountain climbing. Did

27   I tell you about that ninety-six-year old lady who climbed

28   Mount Whitney twice.

29   PAULA: Mother, I do not want to watch TV.

30   MOTHER: Not even "The Young and the Extremely Young."

31   It's my favorite soap. Did I tell you about Lance and

32   Laura?

33   PAULA: *(Getting madder)* Mother!

34   MOTHER: Wait. You'll love this. Lance is having a secret

35   vasectomy so Laura won't get pregnant, but — *(She*

1	*giggles)* **but little does dandy old Lance know that, alas,**
2	**it's too late. Laura is going to have twins!** *(Thinks)* **The**
3	**confusing part is how? She's supposed to be unable to**
4	**have cats in her apartment, let alone twins. Want to**
5	**watch?**
6	**PAULA:** *No! I do not want to watch!*
7	**MOTHER:** *(Putting the TV remote-control unit away)* **I guess this**
8	**is where the parental abuse starts.**
9	**PAULA: Mother, please be reasonable. Please cooperate.**
10	**MOTHER: Paula. Can you hear yourself? You sound like a**
11	**jailer. Please cooperate? What about you cooperating?**
12	**Maybe we can hire another nurse's aide.**
13	**PAULA: No. We've tried everyone in town. You've scared**
14	**them all away. So tomorrow we go to the nursing home.**
15	**MOTHER: I will not.**
16	**PAULA: You will.**
17	**MOTHER: I will not!**
18	**PAULA:** *You will! You will! You will!*
19	**MOTHER: We'll see about that.** *(MOTHER wheels Offstage*
20	*right.)*
21	**PAULA: Mother? Don't do this to me. It's not fair!** *(PAULA*
22	*sits on sofa then lights dim as spotlight comes up on her. Then*
23	*to the audience)* **Well, the next day came and Mother**
24	**completely changed. When it came time to go to the**
25	**nursing home, she went as if she were a good little girl**
26	**going reluctantly off to her first day at school. In the car,**
27	**on the way over to the nursing home, neither of us talked.**
28	*(She stands and as she talks she gets a white sheet from behind*
29	*sofa and covers sofa with it, then gets another one from behind*
30	*sofa and covers TV.)* **When we got there, she just sat silently**
31	**as I signed her in. When the nurse came to take her to**
32	**her room, she went without a fight. It was as easy as that.**
33	*(She takes house keys out of her pocket.)* **I went to her room**
34	**to say goodbye. When it came time for me to leave, I bent**
35	**over to kiss my mother goodbye. And she let me kiss her.**

I hugged her. And she let me hug her. I told her everything would be all right. Then I left. And that was it. That was the day mother left home. It was raining. *(The curtain falls as lights dim and PAULA shrugs and walks Offstage Left. There is the sound of a door slamming shut for the last time.)*

ABOUT THE PLAYWRIGHT

Though still a young man, Robert Mauro has many years of playwriting experience behind his words. His sudden appearance on the theatrical scene as a brilliantly versatile playwright cannot be considered writer's luck. It is position well earned since his childhood days in New York City. It was then that he began creating scenes and playlets.

Unlike many other gifted children who write neighborhood plays for friendly entertainment, Mauro continued his writing into and through his college years winning several regional distinctions and productions. His first adult play was the featured work at Hofstra University's Annual Literary Festival. It launched him into a career as a playwright, writer and editor.

So prolific is Mauro in the wide range of his current writing in a variety of media that he has been required to assume a second pen name.

The publisher of this book believes that Mauro is a talent with a destiny. His works shall most certainly grow in stature and acceptance in American theatre and TV. This collection is but a step along the way.

ORDER FORM

MERIWETHER PUBLISHING LTD.
P.O. BOX 7710
COLORADO SPRINGS, CO 80933
TELEPHONE: (719) 594-4422

Please send me the following books:

_____	**Two Character Plays for Student Actors** **#TT-B174** by Robert Mauro *A collection of 15 one-act plays*	$14.95
_____	**On Stage! Short Plays for Acting Students** **#TT-B165** by Robert Mauro *24 short one-act plays for acting practice*	$12.95
_____	**Theatre Games for Young Performers #TT-B188** by Maria C. Novelly *Improvisations and exercises for developing acting skills*	$12.95
_____	**Winning Monologs for Young Actors** **#TT-B127** by Peg Kehret *Honest-to-life monologs for young actors*	$14.95
_____	**Encore! More Winning Monologs for Young Actors #TT-B144** by Peg Kehret *More honest-to-life monologs for young actors*	$12.95
_____	**The Theatre and You #TT-B115** by Marsh Cassady *An introductory text on all aspects of theatre*	$15.95
_____	**Multicultural Theatre #TT-B205** edited by Roger Ellis *Scenes and monologs by multicultural writers*	$14.95

These and other fine Meriwether Publishing books are available at your local bookstore or direct from the publisher. Use the handy order form on this page.

NAME: _____

ORGANIZATION NAME: _____

ADDRESS: _____

CITY: _____ STATE: _____

ZIP: _____ PHONE: _____

❏ **Check Enclosed**
❏ **Visa or MasterCard #** _____

Signature: _____ *Expiration Date:* _____

(required for Visa/MasterCard orders)

COLORADO RESIDENTS: Please add 3% sales tax.
SHIPPING: Include $2.75 for the first book and 50¢ for each additional book ordered.

❏ *Please send me a copy of your complete catalog of books and plays.*